My Road to Kenya

My Road to Kenya

A Story of Faith, Hope and Democracy in Action

Jack W. O'Leary & Mary Clare Lyons with Virginia Elizabeth Rose

WestBow
PRESS
A DIVISION OF THOMAS NELSON

Copyright © 2012 Jack W. O'Leary & Mary Clare Lyons

All rights reserved. No part of this book may be used or reproduced by any means, graphic, electronic, or mechanical, including photocopying, recording, taping or by any information storage retrieval system without the written permission of the publisher except in the case of brief quotations embodied in critical articles and reviews.

Library of Congress Control Number: 2012911554

WestBow Press books may be ordered through booksellers or by contacting:

WestBow Press
A Division of Thomas Nelson
1663 Liberty Drive
Bloomington, IN 47403
www.westbowpress.com
1-(866) 928-1240

Because of the dynamic nature of the Internet, any web addresses or links contained in this book may have changed since publication and may no longer be valid. The views expressed in this work are solely those of the author and do not necessarily reflect the views of the publisher, and the publisher hereby disclaims any responsibility for them.

Any people depicted in stock imagery provided by Thinkstock are models, and such images are being used for illustrative purposes only.

Certain stock imagery © Thinkstock.

ISBN: 978-1-4497-5662-8 (sc)
ISBN: 978-1-4497-5664-2 (hc)
ISBN: 978-1-4497-5663-5 (e)

Printed in the United States of America

WestBow Press rev. date: 9/4/2012

Dedicated to the people of Kenya who have long struggled for their freedom, and to the priests, nuns, lay people, doctors, nurses and teachers who so selflessly commit to encouraging and helping the Kenyan people as they pursue their dream.

Contents

Acknowledgements ix
Author's Note xi
Foreword xiii
Preface xv

Part I

Chapter 1. Education 1
Chapter 2. Building a Healthy Kenya 16
Chapter 3. Giving Our Best 52
Chapter 4. No One Left Behind 62
Chapter 5. Archbishop Rafael Ndingi of Kenya 80

Part II

Chapter 6. Mary Clare Returns to Kenya 95
Appendix 133
Special Thanks 139
Afterward 143
Epitaph 145
About the Authors 147

Acknowledgements

The trouble with acknowledgements is that you are bound to inadvertently leave out the names of some of those people who did much to help fulfill important commitments and goals. Therefore, I offer my heartfelt thanks to everyone who has worked with us throughout the years without mentioning each and every name.

Many volunteers from organizations ranging from I.M.E.C. to Intervol spent countless hours working to make possible the various projects we undertook.

Beyond our borders, our friends in Kenya volunteered without hesitation, contributing endless hours to ensure that projects came in on budget and were properly completed.

And others donated time and resources, without which we would not have been able to fulfill the promises we made.

Your kindnesses and thoughtfulness are greatly appreciated.

Jack O'Leary

Author's Note

If I could describe in a sentence or two the events I experienced and the lessons I learned through my travels in Kenya, it would be that devastating poverty, combined with tolerance, patience, joy and lots of laughter equal the way of life in Kenya.

I believe that if you were to drift over Kenya in an open-air balloon, besides the lion's roar, you would hear the sound of laughter.

I never intended to become involved in the lives of the people of Kenya. I only went to that far-away country for what was nothing more than a two-week visit. But, little by little, I became drawn in and preoccupied with trying to help in whatever way I could. I knew anything I contributed would only be a drop in the proverbial bucket, but I hoped I would at least be able to make a difference in the lives of some of those in greatest need.

I am writing about some of my adventures as best as I remember them. It is ironic that as I work on what may be my last chapters in Africa, I am flooded with memories of fabulous people I met along the way.

The following is not meant to be a precise documentary of what I experienced throughout many return visits and across many years. I kept no diary and the photographs shown were primarily taken by other people. This is a compilation of my memories and experiences, thoughts and perceptions — both sad and joyous — yet mostly joyous. I wish to share these adventures with those who choose to embark on, what has been for me, a journey of a lifetime.

Jack O'Leary

Foreword

What has been reported as the worst drought on the continent of Africa in sixty years is producing a famine that is spreading throughout Kenya, Ethiopia and Somalia at an alarming rate. Millions of people have been affected and the world's largest refugee camp in Dadaab, Kenya is receiving more than thirteen-hundred people a day from as far away as Somalia. Families who attempt the arduous journey are being attacked by armed rebels and wild animals, and many children never make it to the camp; instead they are dying along the way.

Thirty-seven percent of the population in northern Kenya is suffering from malnutrition due to what is reported to be the world's most severe crop failure in history. The United States government recently announced that the Famine Early Warning System Network has sent out an urgent call throughout the world for food aid.

As an emerging nation, Kenya is also beset with economic and political challenges. Ethnic tensions are growing between the political parties, fueled by campaign rhetoric that precedes the 2013 elections.

A neighboring area recently announced its independence, taking the name South Sudan, resulting in the need for the development of a new currency in order to permit trade between nations. The acquisition of food from the north and oil from the south must now be negotiated. The large Diamond Trust Bank in Kenya has already revised its lending rate upward to an exorbitant 15.75 percent.

However, President Mwai Kibaki has extensive government experience, having served under former President Daniel Moi. He is a well respected economist with clean and honest attributes —much needed in these turbulent times. His main task is to consolidate the diverse range of politicians in his government in order to take on the challenges of a struggling economy, the ravages of a devastating famine and unimaginable ethnic violence.

Attention is being given to the country from a variety of sources. The United Nations is appealing for contributions to cope with the famine, while German Chancellor Angela Merkel has committed 140-million Euros to improve Kenya's infrastructure. The German Delegation Office for Industry and Commerce also has been established in Nairobi to enhance economic ties between the two countries.

With regard to the Catholic Church, there are twenty-two dioceses and thirty-nine bishops in Kenya, ministering to the spiritual and temporal needs of the country's 7.5 million Catholics, which account for 33 percent of the nation's population. The Roman Catholic Church is growing faster in Africa than anywhere else in the world. From 1900 to 2000, the Church in Africa grew from one million to one-hundred and thirty-nine million Catholics. Much attention is being given by church hierarchy to ethnic violence, which has grown out of the nation's abject poverty and territorial tribalism.

Today, Kenyan children are back in school, thanks to President Kibaki, and the people now believe multi-party factions can come together and unite the country with support of the international community: support that ranges from global governmental aid to donations from multi-national corporations, to the generosity and caring of individual philanthropists such as Jack O'Leary and Mary Clare Lyons — people who are committed to restoring hope in the lives of the people of Kenya.

Jack Freeze

Jack Freeze is a retired Engineering Fellow from John Hopkins University and a former adjunct professor at the United States Naval Academy. He is author of two historical novels, *They Shall be Remembered* and *They Left Us Behind*.

Preface

Perhaps he knew as I did not, that the earth was made round so that we would not be far down the road.
Karen Beecher

More than thirty years ago, Basilian priest Charles Lavery, president of St. John Fisher College in Rochester, New York, asked local businessman Jack O'Leary to assist in setting up a fund to help pay tuition for Kenyan priests to study at the college while experiencing American democracy first hand.

President Lavery believed that providing the opportunity for Kenyan priests to earn their advanced degrees while living in America would better prepare them for roles in leadership when they returned to their own country. This, he believed, could help stem the tide of advancing communism in Africa. Somalia and Ethiopia had already fallen to communism, and neighboring Kenya was the next country at risk.

In the years since the scholarship program was established, more than forty Kenyan priests have graduated from undergraduate and graduate school thanks to the kindness extended to them by the Basilian fathers and St. John Fisher College, as well as individuals in Rochester, New York.

All but one scholarship recipient has returned to live and work in Kenya. Another priest who studied at The College at Brockport, State University of New York, Father George Okoth, is a captain in the United States military, where he is working as a chaplain. He served one tour of duty in Iraq and one tour in Germany. Recently, he left for Afghanistan where he will continue to serve American men and women in the military.

In 1993, Jack took his company public and then sold it in 1997. Shortly thereafter, he made his first visit to Kenya. Since then, much of the proceeds from the sale of the company have funded various projects in the country that has so much need, so much poverty, so much sickness.

Jack has used much of his own money to build and/or refurbish hospitals, clinics, dispensaries, churches and schools. With the aid of friends, he built an orphanage for handicapped children and even helped develop a working tea farm.

But his work is not yet done. He recently completed plans to build more orphanages that will provide homes for some of the more than one-million orphans living in danger and hunger on the streets of cities, towns, and villages throughout Kenya. In East Africa, more children have been orphaned than in World War I and World War II combined. Today the enemy of these children is not bullets or bombs; today their enemy is the invisible killer AIDS.

Jack's travels in Kenya led him across formidable landscapes to face endless challenges. They also introduced him to some of the most hospitable, loving and friendly people he has ever known. His adventures also meant the beginning of many cherished memories and lifelong friendships.

As a result of his work on behalf of the people of Kenya, Jack received an education of his own — an education in African corruption. He developed skill and expertise, which have served him well in meeting the challenges of "doing business" with corrupt port authority employees, government officials, and others who would block the delivery of life-saving supplies in order to further their own financial gains.

He accomplished many of his goals — rebuilding hospitals and clinics, and providing medical supplies to help heal the sick. In one area of the country known as Bahati, the infant mortality rate dropped by 80 percent as a result of building just one clinic. Through it all Jack never cursed the darkness; instead he chose to light a candle that continues to shine brightly, bringing hope to the hearts of a spirited and loving people.

Although he never intended to become so intimately involved in the lives of his African friends, he acquired a deep desire to make a difference in their lives and the lives of others. Herein Jack shares in his own words his amazing Kenyan journey.

Mary Clare Lyons

Part I

Major Project Sites as of the End of 2011

Major projects sites include:

Bahati	Nakuru
Bungoma	Neema Medical Center
Eldoret	Soy
Homa Bay	Sindo
Nairobi	

Approximately eighty hospitals and healthcare facilities were recipients of medical supplies and twenty facilities received medical equipment. Not all locations are mentioned herein. This map represents only a few projects completed as of the end of 2011.

Chapter 1
Education

The Foundation of Democracy

My first association with Kenya began in the late 1970s when my friend Father Charles Lavery, then president of St. John Fisher College, asked me to help fund tuition for Kenyan priests he wished to bring to the College. The primary goal was to bring Kenyan priests with proven leadership abilities to the United States to further their education and provide them with the opportunity to experience democracy in action.

The two countries just north of Kenya — Ethiopia and Somalia — had fallen to communist regimes. Father Lavery believed that a working democracy in Kenya could potentially thwart the further spread of communism into East Africa.

Father Lavery envisioned educated and capable Kenyans making a difference in their country after returning home following their studies in the United States.

As a result of the generosity of St. John Fisher College, Father Lavery's dream has materialized. Today, many Kenyan priests have earned their graduate degrees at Fisher and other Rochester area colleges, going home with their degrees in hand and the real-life experience of living in a democratic society.

Since returning to their homeland, their influence has spread over much of East Africa. Of the more than forty priests taking part in the program, six of the graduates have expanded their leadership roles in their communities and have gone on to become Bishops in Kenya's Catholic Church.

One of the first graduates, Father Rafael Ndingi, who later became the Archbishop of Nairobi, is committed to freedom for his nation and its people. Since returning to Kenya, Father Ndingi has lived a life of danger, fighting corruption in government and working for honest elections. He has been instrumental in laying the groundwork for a coalition government which has helped to prevent the fighting and civil unrest that normally erupts during national elections. His intellect, abilities as a negotiator and undying commitment to the people of Kenya have formed a foundation upon which the people can stand in hope for their country's political unity.

I did not have sufficient funds to be of much help to Father Lavery when he first asked me to support his scholarship program. Instead, I was able to give him stock in a new company that I was helping to start in Amherst, New York. After the company, IIMAK Inc., went public, the college was able to sell its shares. Half of the profits were used to set up a scholarship for tuition, the other half were used to create a fund that would make money available to the graduates to use upon their return to Kenya.

The first group of Kenyan priests to come to Rochester lived either in the Basilian House of Studies, the home for Basilian priests who taught at Fisher, or Becket Hall, which, at that time, was occupied by Bishop Joseph Hogan of the Rochester Diocese.

Father Rafael Ndingi lived with Bishop Hogan, whose generosity went beyond sharing his living accommodations with the Kenyan priest. Bishop Hogan knew Father Ndingi had never before experienced such harsh and frigid weather conditions as those that accompany a Western New York winter and that he was ill prepared for the months of cold ahead. And so he purchased much-needed winter clothing and other necessities for Father Ndingi.

Years later, when Father Ndingi returned for a visit to the Rochester area, he returned not as Father Ndingi, but as Archbishop Ndingi. He was traveling with his secretary, Father Stephen Mbugua Ngari, another St. John Fisher College graduate. As we drove by St. John Fisher College and Becket Hall, the Archbishop pointed out his former home. A man of integrity, he explained that while at Fisher he had an arrangement with Bishop Hogan's secretary whereby she would type his school papers but not make any corrections. All mistakes, even spelling errors, were to be typed as they were written.

As usual, Father Stephen, who has a great sense of humor and loves to exaggerate, chirped in, telling the Bishop, "Today you do not have to worry about spelling errors. You just type on a word processor and at the end you push a button and all mistakes are corrected."

The Bishop looked to me for confirmation. He asked, "Is this true, Mr. O'Leary?" "Yes, for the most part it is," I answered. He pondered this for a moment and then confidently pronounced, "It sounds like cheating to me!"

Living with the Basilian fathers was a great aid to the Kenyan priests who were provided free room and board. However, they had no income or health insurance. So we worked out a new plan. They would live in various parishes in the Rochester area and serve these parishes as assistant pastors. In exchange, the Kenyan priests would receive a small salary and health insurance. Often someone in the parish would lend their assistant pastor a car for transportation. On the whole, this program worked out very well, and in many cases even better than imagined. Relationships that would last a lifetime often developed between priest and parishioner.

Many times the Kenyan priests would spend holidays at my home in Rochester. Among my most memorable recollections of these shared holidays is the time when Father Stephen asked if he could invite Kenyan Masai priest, Father Simon, to join us for dinner.

To add to the excitement of the festivities, Father Stephen took it upon himself to convince my wife Peggy that Masai priests had a few dietary restrictions. Specifically, he convinced her that one particular priest only ate his meat raw. He expanded upon his story by claiming that the priest did not partake in drinking wine, adding that the priest's tribe drank blood and suggested his red wine glass be filled with blood.

My wife Peggy was very capable at organizing dinners, garden parties and events for all occasions, including graduation parties for many of the Kenyan priests. But this was a situation she'd never before encountered. Somewhat in a panic, she inquired as to where one would purchase fresh blood. Father Stephen suggested she pick up a few pints at the butcher shop. Then, satisfied with his story, Stephen announced it was time for him to leave. He said his good-byes and I walked him to the door.

It wasn't long before the angry voice of my wife was loudly summoning me to the kitchen. While I was trying to convince my wife that Father Stephen's story was a hoax, I'm sure that Stephen was laughing and enjoying his practical joke all the way home.

Another memorable Thanksgiving highlight came when Father Stephen asked on a Thanksgiving morning if he could bring five additional Kenyan guests to join us for dinner. Of course, we welcomed our additional guests.

Gathering around the dinner table, one of our guests asked if he could carve the bird because he had never before seen such a large turkey. With carving set in hand, he skillfully operated on the bird.

My youngest son Brian whispered to his brother Michael, "I know Dad said that the guy with the knife is a priest, but if he yells 'zulu! zulu!' I'm out of here." Brian was making reference to William Faure's epic tale *Shaka Zulu,* an account of the life of that fearsome warrior who, as leader of the Zulu tribe of South Africa, had spread terror while earning the respect of the people living within a thousand miles of his epic battles. Shaka Zulu had formed one of the greatest light infantries of all time. When attacking their enemies, Zulu's warriors would chant "zulu, zulu."

Throughout the years of adventure and laughter, my family and I forged deep friendships with many of these priests who had come to America to study and prepare for important roles of leadership in their homeland.

After I retired from my job at IIMAK, Inc., I had more time to travel and was delighted that I could now visit my friends in their country, Kenya.

And thus began an adventure — one that, if given the opportunity to do all over again, I would do so in a heartbeat. My life and theirs will be forever joined, forged together by shared experiences, mutual esteem, love, and much laughter.

From Trash to Treasure

One of the first projects that we undertook for the people of Kenya was in 1991 and was inspired by Mary Clare Lyons' youngest daughter Kathleen.

Education is the key to opening doors that lead a nation out of poverty, famine, ignorance and the bondage of superstition. Yet, many schools in Kenya lack even minimal resources necessary for educating the nation's children.

Hearing about the children of Kenya who were without school books or basic school supplies, Kathleen turned to her mother and said, "We can send them books."

Kathleen wasted no time getting started on her mission. Sitting down at the family computer, she composed a letter, which she sent to nearby school districts. She addressed the envelopes, stuffed them with her request for castoff school books, then sealed the envelopes to be mailed the following day.

Perhaps it was a mother's instinct at work, but for whatever reason, Mary Clare decided to check the letter one last time after Kathleen had gone to bed. It was a good thing she did! Relying on spell check for a last review to be sure the letters were perfect, Kathleen had closed the letter, "Sensually yours, Kathleen." Mary Clare unsealed the envelopes, changed the closing on the letters to read, "Sincerely yours, Kathleen," and restuffed and resealed the envelopes, never telling her daughter about the intervention.

And so, early that summer Mary Clare, her daughters and her mom made trip after trip to school districts throughout the area, filling their cars with first hundreds and then thousands of books. Soon, Mary

Clare's two-and-one-half-car garage was stacked high with pallets of books.

Initially, more than five-thousand textbooks were collected. The books were sorted by subject and grade level then boxed for shipping to a distribution point in Nakuru, Kenya. From there, the books were redistributed to their final destinations; much to the delight of the teachers, librarians, and boys and girls who would use them.

Of course, it wasn't quite that easy. As with all of our projects for Kenya, we first had some obstacles to overcome.

After the initial contact with the school districts, Mary Clare (a schoolteacher herself at the time) and I had conversations with one school administrator after another. All gave the same response. Each would be happy to give us their district's or school's new or gently used books slated for disposal at the end of the school year. However, the schools were not at liberty to give away the no-longer usable books.

To our surprise, we learned there was a New York State law that specified any unneeded books, new or used, could not be given away to charities. The reason was because they had been purchased with taxpayer money. Giving the books to any specific charity or organization would be a form of favoritism and, therefore, unlawful. So the books had to be discarded and most likely would be hauled away to landfills.

In discussing this wastefulness with a friend of ours, she decided to do some research on the matter, which revealed an interesting fact. She learned that in 1988 the United States Supreme Court ruled in California vs. Greenwood that garbage left curbside is no longer private property. The result of the ruling was that those perfectly usable books being discarded in dumpsters were considered "free for the taking."

Thankfully, when they heard about the Supreme Court ruling, some enterprising principals told us, "Well, I cannot give them to you, but I can tell you that the books we're disposing of will be in boxes sitting next to the dumpster at 10 a.m. next Tuesday. If you happen to see boxes marked "books" next to the dumpster, what happens to them is no longer our business. If the boxes turn up missing, I will simply presume they were discarded."

Variations on this scenario occurred from one school district to another. We started by collecting books discarded by just four local districts, which, in the end, turned out to be in the thousands. I couldn't begin to imagine the many, many books being discarded by all the school districts throughout the state. It was difficult to believe that anyone could condone, let alone conceive of such waste.

Mary Clare and her daughters spent days picking up the more than five-thousand textbooks sitting next to dumpers at schools throughout the area. If new, and many were, we estimate the books would have been valued at more than $400,000.

That summer, the better part of Mary Clare's two-and-one-half-car garage was filled with books collected from districts as far as twenty-five miles from her home.

After first being sorted by grade level and then by subject, and with complete sets of books for every grade level compiled, the books were carefully boxed and inventoried, and the necessary packing lists were attached. In the last innings of the collection process, we learned that specific science and math books were also needed by schools in Kenya. So we set to work locating these books and preparing them for shipment.

As with all of our Kenya projects, it seemed that once a project was identified and the work involved to complete it began, people stepped forward to make donations or to help in whatever way they could. This was also true with the book project. Hearing about the Kenya Book Project, teachers and librarians in the area forwarded to Mary Clare additional precious texts slated for destruction by their own institutions.

The summer we collected, packed and shipped the textbooks turned out to be one of the hottest summers ever to hit Upstate New York. It was so hot in fact that Mary Clare feared her garage would catch fire due to the sun's heat igniting the thousands of stored textbooks and sparking a spontaneous combustion blaze. She decided it would be prudent to install air conditioning in her garage. The air conditioning reduced the potential of a fire breaking out and was much appreciated by the workers who toiled through the summer heat and humidity to complete our project.

When we finally had all the books ready to go, I borrowed a truck, we loaded up the books, and I drove the truck to IIMAK.

Volunteers convened in Mary Clare's garage on a hot summer day to help pack and then load books into the truck that would take them on the next leg of their journey. Book packers from left: Jack, Father Stephen, Kathleen, Chuck and Father Paul.

A former coworker of mine volunteered to help us by completing the paperwork required for international shipping, which was a considerable task.

Soon after the books shipped, I received my first lesson in African corruption. Upon arrival at the Port of Mombasa, the books were held up for "inspection." As time went by, fees accrued, additional charges were levied, and expenses rose. When I arrived in Kenya a few months later, I was surprised to learn that the books were still at the port.

Together, Father Stephen and I went to customs to get the books released. I stepped up to the counter and explained to the customs agent my problem with getting the books released. I felt like I was having the unusual experience of talking to the long-departed baseball great Casey Stengel, manager of the New York Yankees, who liked to confuse reporters by speaking gibberish, which became known as Stengelese. He always spoke very seriously and with a straight face while conjuring up his own make-believe words that made no sense whatsoever.

The customs agent looked right past me, speaking in what sounded to me like Stengelese. Turning to Father Stephen, I told him I had no idea what the agent was saying.

"He wants a bribe," Father Stephen replied. And I knew there was no alternative. I paid $1,500 to the corrupt customs agent and the books were finally released.

Students throughout Kenya happily receive new school books.

We later found a better way to ship books to avoid these problems in the future. We learned that the United States Post Office would send up to sixty pounds of boxed books to a third-world country for just one dollar per pound if the books were brought to the Post Office in postal canvas mail sacks commonly known as M bags.

Using this method, we shipped specifically requested books to a number of different schools and libraries. Medical books were of particular value to healthcare clinics and hospitals.

The books were boxed and then placed into the M bags, which were given to us in advance by the U.S. Post Office. Each bag of books had to be processed at the front counter of the local post office by a postal clerk. When the clerks first saw us standing in line with dozens of sixty-pound bags of books, their jaws dropped. But much to their credit, when they realized what we were doing, they rolled up their sleeves and completed the required mountain of paperwork.

Father Stephen Comes to Rochester

Father Stephen Mbugua came to Rochester in the 1980s to attend St. John Fisher College. He then went on to receive a master's degree at the Rochester Institute of Technology. During his stay, we became close friends.

Sarah Brewin, a registered nurse who lives in Massachusetts and who became an invaluable partner in our Kenyan projects, said to me, "Every time I am with Stephen, I just laugh."

But Stephen also has his serious side as well. Since returning to Kenya following his schooling in Rochester, Father Stephen has been pastor of two parishes, a principal at a boys school, and a psychology teacher at Egerton University in Nakuru, Kenya. After authoring a textbook on psychology, he was made dean of the university's School of Psychology.

Before my first trip to Africa to visit with Father Stephen, he contacted me in Rochester, asking if I would help him build a church.

He explained that the church he grew up in as a child in Mlima, Kenya was a dilapidated, mud-walled, thatched-roof building. Despite its crumbling structure, parishioners still faithfully attended mass there. So Stephen, others and I joined forces and built the new church, which was named St. Paul's. He did such a good job as general contractor on that job I asked him to be my advisor on future projects.

Jack visits St. Paul's Church in Mlima with Father Stephen.

My Road to Kenya

With all of Father Stephen's skills, one thing he is not is a safari guide. I was warned by mutual friend Judy Graper not to go into game preserves with Father Stephen. Despite these warnings, I couldn't resist joining him in his private automobile on a personally guided tour through Nakuru National Park.

When on safari, it is imperative that one adheres to certain guidelines and rules for their own personal safety.

Rule Number One: When you enter a game preserve, you must leave your car and travel in a vehicle built for such travels and driven exclusively by a trained safari driver. This is one rule from which no one is exempt, no one it seems except Father Stephen.

This rule evidently did not apply to Stephen because, arriving at the game preserve, Stephen drove right through the gate and into the park as if he was one of the official safari guides. Once inside the preserve, he proceeded to forge a trail of his own through the park.

His first antic was to drive down a narrow path that was completely closed in by bush growing up on either side. Evidently Stephen knew that lions were in the habit of using this path and he wanted to goad one of them into jumping onto the hood of his vehicle. Soon he located a lion on the path and Stephen, shall we say, invited the lion to climb aboard our car. With a long graceful leap the lion jumped onto the hood of the car and stared at us through the windshield, the only barrier between us and the curious cat. When he was ready to move along, Stephen blew the horn and the lion jumped off the car and disappeared into the bush!

Rule Number Two: Remain in your vehicle at all times. As long as you stay in your safari car, you are safe from any animals living in the park except for the occasional elephant. Stephen essentially ignored this rule as well.

From our vehicle, we viewed a water buffalo standing about one-hundred yards away. Obviously, the only thing to do was to get out of the car and take a closer look.

We edged closer, but the water buffalo refused to budge. It would not come any closer to us. Instead, it just remained where it was and stared at us. For some reason, I thought it would be a good idea to get the pillow from the back seat of Stephen's car so that Stephen could wave it at the buffalo as some sort of signal or sign that would draw the animal to us.

Like a matador in a bull fight, Stephen waved and waved the brightly colored pillow, trying to get a reaction out of the buffalo, but still the animal refused to budge. Seemingly indifferent, it just stood staring in our direction. I wonder what it thought of two grown men madly waiving a pillow at it. It seemed to me the animal was nothing if not bored with these crazy men standing in the grass waving a pillow as if this was an everyday occurrence. Unconcerned, and not even amused, the buffalo finally turned and walked away.

We returned to the car and after a while decided for some reason that it would be another good idea if we took a walk. Leading the way, Stephen went out ahead of me. I quickly lost sight of him and was soon wandering around on my own, looking for him and feeling a little bit uncomfortable.

During my search for Stephen, I came upon the half-eaten carcass of some unfortunate creature. As I looked at the remains, my one thought was, "Is this all that is left of Stephen?" I hoped that whatever had eaten him had not also swallowed the car keys, which were in Stephen's pocket. Eventually our paths crossed and we joyfully headed home.

On another safari with him, I decided I could get better pictures of the animals if I sat on top of the safari truck. A game warden soon caught up with us and told me to get back inside the truck, explaining that jackals and lions can easily jump as high as the truck's roof top. I complied, climbing back inside the truck. But once we lost the game warden, I again climbed out of the vehicle. Unfortunately, the warden soon found us again. This time he said to me, "If you get out of your vehicle one more time, I will shoot you." I stayed in the truck.

My Road to Kenya

A view of Jack sitting atop a jeep photographing animals on safari as he must have looked through the game warden's scope.

Somebody Up There Likes Brother Martin

The chessboard is the world; the pieces are the phenomena of the universe. Thomas Huxley

Some time ago, a Kenyan named Brother Martin Okongo arrived in Rochester. He had heard about St. John Fisher College and the scholarships that were available to Kenyan priests. It appeared that he made the trip on faith alone as he had not applied for either admission to the College or for one of the scholarships. He also neglected to notify anyone that he was coming.

Normally the Kenyan priests would not just show up on the doorstep of St. John Fisher College thinking they were all set to attend fall classes. Among other things, a completed and accepted application and letters of recommendation from the priest's Bishop were required.

Brother Martin knew nothing at all about the standard college application process. Never before had he completed a college application or received an acceptance letter. So one day, out of the blue, Brother

Martin just showed up at the college. He explained to the admissions counselors that his order of brothers had no accounting system and that he wished to set up one, once he completed his degree in accounting. Somehow the college was able to work things out and he was immediately admitted with a full scholarship to study accounting.

Once again, the Basilian Fathers in Rochester pitched in and provided Martin with free room and board while he was at the school. The first summer after he started school I asked Martin if he would like a job in my company in Buffalo and he said "yes."

The plan was for Martin to ride back and forth to Buffalo with me every day — about seventy miles each way. This arrangement worked well for a short time, but after about a week or so I thought about what would happen when I was out of town on business. I would be unable to drive Martin back and forth between Rochester and Buffalo, and there was no place in Buffalo where he could stay.

I asked my secretary to call the closest Catholic church to find out the name of the pastor and to get me his phone number. Later I called the parish and spoke to Monsignor William McDonnell.

After speaking briefly with one another, he asked if I was the Jack O'Leary he had sat with at a United Way dinner party a few weeks prior. I told him that, in fact, I was the very same Jack O'Leary. What an amazing coincidence. I had no idea we had met a few weeks earlier. He is the only priest I ever met in Buffalo. I told him about Brother Martin and mentioned he needed a place in Buffalo to live for the summer. He asked us to visit him that afternoon.

We arrived at St. Leo the Great Catholic Church later that day and the priest greeted us at the door of the rectory. He asked Martin where he was from. Martin answered, "I am from Kenya." Father asked him just where in Kenya would that be. Martin answered, "Nairobi." Father asked, "Did you ever know Bishop John McCarthy before he passed away?" With a broad smile, Martin replied, "Bishop McCarthy is the man who founded our order. I knew him very well." The coincidence was uncanny. Not only was this the only priest I had ever met in Buffalo, but the two men — one Kenyan, one American — shared a common friend.

Monsignor McDonnell escorted us to his sitting room where a chess board sat on a table between two chairs. He told us Bishop McCarthy often visited the United States to raise funds for his projects in Kenya. When he was done with his fundraising efforts, he would visit this very same parish to rest. The coincidences continued. The former pastor of St. Leos was from Dublin, Ireland, and had been ordained on the same day as Bishop McCarthy. Whenever the Bishop visited the parish, the two friends played chess together, sitting opposite one another at this very table.

The pastor explained that if they were in the middle of a game when it was time for Bishop McCarthy to leave, they left the chess board as it sat until Bishop McCarthy returned on his next trip to the United States. Sometimes Bishop McCarthy would not return for three or four years, but the board remained untouched until the friends once again came together to match skills. He went on to tell us that probably no one would ever touch the chessboard again as both men had died.

He then took us to the second floor and unlocked one of the doors lining the hallway and said, "Martin, this will be your room." He gave Martin the keys to the bedroom door and we returned to the main floor where he gave Martin a set of keys to the front door, saying, "Martin, you can come and go as you please, and you are welcome to join us for meals anytime you are in the building."

When I returned to my office, I called Paul Batt, owner of a Buick dealership where IIMAK, Inc. leased all the company's vehicles. I asked Paul if he could loan Martin a car for a few months so he could get back and forth to work and to the University of Buffalo for night classes. Paul gave Martin a next-to-new Buick Regal. The only contract was a handshake between the two men.

That weekend Martin drove back to Rochester in his new car and met his friend Father Stephen who was driving an old junker someone had provided him. After he saw Martin's new car and found out he had a great place to live, a job in IIMAK's accounting department and was attending the University of Buffalo, Stephen shook his head and smiled a grin from ear to ear, saying, "Martin, somebody up there likes you."

Chapter 2
Building a Healthy Kenya

One Community at a Time

After Kenya gained independence from Great Britain in 1964, many of the English farmers left the country. Most of their English-design farms were too large for single families to purchase and work on their own. As a result, cooperatives were formed by hundreds of families pooling their resources to buy one large farm. The families then divided the land into hundreds of small, manageable farms.

Generally speaking, the English farmhouses were no longer of any use since they were too big and costly to maintain. Many of these beautiful homes were abandoned and it didn't take long before they fell into disrepair.

The cooperative owners of one of these large homes formed a plan to save the stately house while helping the people living in the area. The cooperative promised it would donate the home to Father Stephen's parish on one condition — that he convert it into a hospital to serve the healthcare needs of the local community. Father Steven accepted the challenge and reached out to me for whatever help I could offer.

Although Father Stephen's parish was Roman Catholic, religious affiliations were never a factor in this project. The purpose of this plan was to provide a medical facility to serve all members of the community, regardless of their faith or ability to pay.

My Road to Kenya

There were many hurdles to overcome in rehabbing the building from farmhouse to medical facility, but from the beginning we decided we would build while embracing Nelson Mandela's message, "It always seems impossible until it is done."

I was informed there were fifty-five-thousand people living in the area surrounding Bahiti and that healthcare was virtually inaccessible to them all. The mortality rate was particularly high for children in the Bahati area with many dying from curable or preventable diseases, including dysentery and malaria.

With almost no roads — paved or otherwise — and with the only other medical facility a long bus ride to Nakuru once you did make it to the main road, not many made the journey. Although Nakuru was no more than thirty miles away, there was little or no means to get there.

Travel in Kenya at that time was difficult by any standard. Most buses in Kenya are not as we know them in the West. Most of Kenya's buses were and continue to be Volkswagen vans built to hold about sixteen people. Ten years ago these vans typically carried twenty-five to thirty passengers at a time. Once the interior of a bus was filled beyond capacity, it was common for people to climb up on top and make their journey sitting on the van's roof. Obviously, this was no way to transport a person who was seriously ill. Today in Kenya it is illegal to overload buses and vans.

Father Stephen told me how much it would cost to turn the house into the medical facility that he planned to name St. John's Cottage Hospital, and I agreed to finance the project. He immediately went to work, preparing to bring medical care to the people of Bahati.

One of the early hurdles we overcame prior to establishing the hospital was to bring electrical service to the area. To the best of my knowledge, the closest service available at that time was at a small nearby army post. We contacted the government, inquiring about the possibility of extending the power lines to the hospital. After some financial negotiations, an agreement was made and the government connected the hospital to the army post's power line.

The English farmhouse before its transformation into a hospital.

St. John's Cottage Hospital under renovation.

Jack visits the newly opened St. John's Cottage Hospital.

My Road to Kenya

When the conversion of the farm house into St. John's Cottage Hospital was completed, a forty-foot container of medical equipment was shipped from the United States. It included, among other things, a birthing center, an operating room, a ward for women and children, and a modest laboratory for testing for infectious diseases.

Although St. John's Cottage Hospital was designed to provide only basic healthcare, it serves a wide geographic area. With just twelve beds available, most patients and expectant mothers are provided care through the hospital's outpatient services.

I was told recent studies have concluded that the child mortality rate in the area decreased by eighty percent since St. John's Cottage Hospital became operational. These results were achieved primarily because of the introduction of a sterile birthing facility, the lab that could successfully detect simple infections, and the treatment of dysentery, pneumonia and malaria.

After St. John's Cottage Hospital was completed, a celebration with an open house and Catholic mass was held. Father Stephen assisted Bishop Peter Nyeri in celebrating the mass at a nearby church, which is called an "outlying church." Priests use these outlying churches to celebrate Sunday mass for the people in the area. Because there was no electricity in the church, all services were held during daylight hours, allowing time for worshipers to walk home safely after services.

Most parishes in Kenya have outlying churches. After a priest says mass at his main parish, he travels to the outlying churches to celebrate mass as long as daylight allows. These churches can be up to fifty miles away from the parish church. The priests cannot get to every outlying church every Sunday, so they alternate Sundays between the churches. This system makes it possible for priests to serve the spiritual needs of the people in the areas beyond the towns and villages.

When the hospital opened, lots of dancing, praying and singing of songs intermixed with the celebration's worship services. As the celebration came to a close, the parishioners presented gifts to Father Stephen, Bishop Nyeri, and to me as well. Stephen received a chicken, the Bishop received a rooster with bound feet, and I received a goat presented to me by a young girl who walked up the aisle of the church leading the animal on a short rope leash.

The child smiled with great pride and dignity as she placed the leash in my hand. I was greatly moved by the transfer of ownership of the goat from the girl's family to me because I understood that in Africa it is a great honor to be presented a goat as a gift.

As we prepared to leave the church, it became apparent to me that I could not keep the goat for a pet. Furthermore, the transportation costs and complex logistics of sending the goat to the United States would likewise prove prohibitive. We decided to give all three of the animal gifts to The Little Sisters of St. Francis.

So, without hesitation, Stephen loaded the rooster, the chicken and the goat into the back seat of his car and we drove with our newfound passengers to The Little Sisters of St. Francis.

The order of The Little Sisters of St. Francis is expanding in Uganda and Kenya. Because the diets of the people in the area are limited and nutritional needs are seldom met, the nuns farm their land, growing vegetables to share with those in need. They also raise a few farm animals, such as chickens, goats, pigs and cows.

At one time, The Little Sisters of St. Francis in Kenya asked me to build an industrial chicken coop to provide food and an income source for the novitiate, a group of thirty girls preparing to become nuns. I funded this project and went on my way, hoping our roads would one day cross again.

It was in the United States that Father Stephen introduced me to Sister Agnes, another member of The Little Sisters of St. Francis order. That was a quarter of a century ago. Stephen was returning to Kenya when Sister Agnes arrived in Rochester from Kenya.

I learned that Sister Agnes's real name is Margaret W. Walubuka, but that it was changed somewhere along the way to Sister Agnes.

Although Sister had limited means, she possessed great inner strength and a vibrant spirit. She told Stephen she wished to earn a master's degree at the Rochester Institute of Technology National Institute for the Deaf, but somehow her scholarship, which had been in place when she had left Kenya, was no longer available.

To get a scholarship to the National Institute for the Deaf is no easy task. But with the help of two friends, Al Simone, president of Rochester Institute of Technology, and Don Lennox, for whom the school had named its Don Lennox Center, Sister was able to accomplish her goal of earning her master's degree and went on to put her great tenacity and strong management skills to work building five homes for handicapped adults in Virginia.

She is a woman of great faith and strength, and has a special ability for influencing others to work toward their own goals.

Recently, Sister Agnes also received a license to service handicapped adults in a daycare capacity in Virginia. One day Sister will return to Kenya to be with her order.

As many chapters of her story are still unfolding, I wanted to share Sister Agnes' life story, which is one of spirit, tenacity and success. She is one of the most tenacious people I have ever met. She is an inspiration to me, and because I know she has positive impact on everyone she meets, I placed her story in a downloadable format at www.myroadtokenya.com.

Life with Father Stephen is Always an Adventure

One time when I went to Kenya to inspect the progress on some projects, I stayed with Father Stephen at his house. After my stay, I had the thought that instead of spending a lot of money on a fancy safari trip tourists should stay with Stephen. This would prove to be far more interesting and exciting than your run-of-the-mill safari. Adventurers could go on a private safari with Stephen as driver and guide, while also witnessing the comings and goings of Stephen's daily life, which I believe would make for an excellent reality TV show!

Something as simple as shopping with Stephen is an experience in itself. Imagine making a visit to the general store on Main Street in Nakuru. Since there is no parking garage, nor parking spaces, you are forced to park either in the street or on the sidewalk. Sometimes cars are parked facing forward, while other times they are sideways, backwards, and just about every which way without any semblance of order. It was constant gridlock on Main Street, but no one seemed to take notice or care.

During one excursion, we made our way through the maze of parked cars, and entered the general store where I purchased a bottle of gin, tonic water, and ice cube trays. Ice cubes are a bit of an anomaly in Kenya, where the people generally consume their beverages at room temperature. I, however, was determined to have a nice cold drink that evening. But doing so would prove a bit more difficult than I thought.

Returning to Stephen's house, I filled the ice cube trays with bottled water, placed them in the freezer compartment of Steven's refrigerator, and then waited for the water to freeze into ice cubes.

A few hours later I went to the freezer to see how my cubes were doing. I was surprised to find the water had not yet frozen. So I put the trays back in the freezer and waited a few more hours. When I returned to the kitchen the second time and opened the freezer, I couldn't believe it. Still no ice cubes, just water.

The "Jack of all trades" who worked for Stephen happened to be sitting in the kitchen as I checked the ice cube trays the second time. I asked him if the freezer was working properly. With an inquisitive look on his face, he asked me why I was asking. I explained that the water I placed in the trays was still unfrozen after being in the freezer for several hours.

With eyes wide, he exclaimed, "You wanted the ice!?! When the water got solid, I threw it out and put new water in the tray for you." He added, "I did not know you wanted ice; I thought you just wanted cold water."

The next night we went out to dinner at a golf club where Father Stephen was a member. The bartender's expression was priceless when we each pulled a plastic bag filled with ice cubes out of our pockets and began putting the cubes into our drinks.

I could write an entire book about my adventures with Stephen, but I will tell only a few more stories of the fun we had together.

After dinner one night, while sitting with Father Stephen in his living room, I told him I wanted to take a walk. Stephen said he would have to go with me to introduce me to Paul, the night watchman.

Kenya sits on the equator, so there are twelve hours of daylight and twelve hours of darkness every day of the year. By 7 p.m. it is pitch dark, and as we went outside I noticed it had already grown very dark. Stephen called out for Paul and soon a figure moved in the shadows.

As Paul emerged from the darkness, I thought I was looking at Robinson Crusoe himself stepping out of the pages of the familiar tale. Paul sported a cape made of animal skins that he wore as a poncho tied at the waste with a rope. On his head he wore a homemade leather cap that framed his face and came to a point at the top. A bow and quiver filled with arrows were slung over his shoulder and across his back, and a machete was tucked into his waistband. He carried a steel spear in his hand. The spear was the same type of spear the Masai use to protect their cattle from lions. He was tall, thin, and appeared to be very strong. He may have been a warrior, but I am still not certain about that.

Paul spoke to me, saying, "Do not move while I call the dogs." Then he gave a shout and almost instantly three dogs materialized out of the darkness. Never before had I seen dogs that looked like these three animals. They seemed to be more like large wild coyotes than dogs. They were skinny and their mangy coats were uneven with large patches of fur missing. Each one looked as if it had been in more than a few fights. The animals came closer and Paul said, "Now that they have met you with me, they will never bother you. They will be your friends." I thought, "Thank God I am on their side. I would hate to be their enemy."

Together Paul and I walked the compound. As we walked, we shared a long talk. Despite his untamed appearance, he was an informed and delightful companion. He explained that at the first sign of daylight the dogs were fed a large meal and then, because they were trained to do so, would sleep all day. At dusk they woke up ready for another night's work guarding the compound.

When on duty, the dogs did not stay together as a pack; instead they separated and roamed the grounds on their own, never barking unless they observed something suspicious in their section of the compound. If one sensed something unusual, it barked as a signal to the other two.

Once all the dogs were together, they barked in unison to let Paul know where they were so he could easily locate them.

Most homes of value in Kenya have walls that surround their perimeters, separating them from the outside world. Usually these walls have nails or cut glass embedded at the top to deter intruders. Driveways also are sealed off by large, steel gates.

Paul told me that, using his bow and arrow, he shoots any intruders trying to climb over the fence. "Why not use a gun," I asked. He explained that an arrow is a better choice of weapon because more than one bandit could be climbing over the fence, and they could have guns. "If I shoot them with a gun, they know where I am." Explaining further he said, "Guns create a spark when fired. The spark of light could reveal to the intruders where I am located."

I asked Paul if he ever had to shoot someone with an arrow. He said that, yes, he had done so quite a few times. He told me a few weeks before he had seen a bandit climbing over the wall and had shot him in the thigh with an arrow. Then Paul added, "The bandit was very angry." I thought to myself, "Well that's a surprise." Paul said he could still hear the bandit cursing when he was a long distance away.

Another adventure with Stephen took place over something as simple as toast for breakfast.

A typical breakfast at Stephen's home consists of tea, a type of oatmeal, and toast and butter. The bread in Kenya is delicious and I always looked forward to toast with my breakfast each morning. One morning there was no toast.

Stephen explained that the toaster was not working and he had to call the toaster repairman. I could not believe there was any such thing as a toaster repairman, but a few hours later the toaster repairman rode up to the house on a bicycle, the tools of his trade carrying in a basket. After taking a look at the toaster, the repairman announced that although he could fix it, the toaster was on its last leg. He repaired the toaster, charging only fifty cents for the service.

That afternoon, Stephen and I went to the city of Nakuru. I asked him to stop at the general store because I wanted to buy him a new toaster. When we arrived at the store, I told him I was going to kid the young lady at the counter and asked that he go along with the joke.

I explained to the store clerk that I would like a new type of toaster that I saw in the United States. I continued, "It has three buttons on the front. If you are at one end of the table and the toaster is at the other, and if you press button one, the toaster shoots the toast about four feet to the other end of the table. Now, if the toaster is on the kitchen counter and you press button two, the toaster shoots the toast across the room to where you are sitting at the table. Now, the third button is for eating outdoors on the patio. Hit the third button and the toaster shoots the toast right through the open window all the way to your patio table." I asked, "Do you carry toasters like that?"

Without as much as cracking a smile, she said, "Yes, but I just sold the last one this morning. Would you like a more conventional toaster?" I replied, "That would be fine."

Hearing this interchange between the clerk and myself, Stephen howled with laughter. As we left the store, Stephen, still chuckling, remarked, "She got you good."

On my next visit to Kenya, Stephen and I returned to the same general store where I bought him another toaster and a new microwave oven. Stephen had given his microwave and toaster to the Bishop.

Doing What it Takes to Run a Tea Farm

I am dealing with things as they come along.
Lucinda Williams

Some years ago, I learned the Diocese of Nairobi was in the process of revitalizing a former English tea plantation on land it owned and that equipment to work the farm was needed. Mainly they needed a large tractor, and I was happy to provide one.

The project was planned by Archbishop Rafael Ndingi, one of the original St. John Fisher College graduates. The Archbishop told me he put one of the diocesan nuns in charge of the entire operation. No one believed she could do the difficult job that was ahead of her. But his judgment proved to be correct and eventually even the biggest naysayers agreed the energetic nun was doing an excellent job of managing the farm.

I returned to Kenya years later and made it a point to revisit the tea farm. By now the tea was ready for harvesting. Sister escorted me on a tour of the grounds, and I was impressed to see that everything at the farm was neat, clean and organized. The day I was at the farm I saw at least fifty women enthusiastically picking the tea leaves. Sister told me most of these women were the primary supporters of their families. If not for the tea farm, these families would be in desperate straights.

Walking up and down the rows and rows of plants, Sister taught me how to pick the tea leaves. As we made our way down a neatly planted furrow, Sister, walking beside me and carrying a large basket on her back, stopped in front of each plant expertly removing the valuable leaves. I marveled time and again as Sister skillfully selected the choicest of leaves from the tops of the shrubs and, with both hands in motion, threw them over her shoulder into the basket behind her. She explained it took about a half of a day to fill just one basket.

When filled, the tea baskets were taken to a station for weighing and payment was made to the picker. When the tea was ready for transport to a nearby processing plant, it was carried there in a cart pulled by the tractor.

At the processing plant, the tea leaves were spread out on large tarps and left for several days to air dry. Then the green leaves were heated until they turned a deep, rich brown.

Some of the tea leaves were then finely ground for instant tea, and others were chopped, packaged and sealed into tea bags. Once packaged, the tea was ready to be shipped to customers.

Sister was later transferred back to her old post as an administrator in the Diocesan Center in Nairobi, and a young man from Milan, Italy came to Kenya to run the plantation for the Diocese. Gabriele Beacco, an Italian standing six feet, three inches tall, was an accountant who had tired of his desk job crunching numbers in Italy. He decided running a tea farm in Kenya would be a good change of pace.

Usually, you would hear Gabriele long before he came into view. From a distance you could hear him signing Verdi at the top of his lungs.

Walking the farm or driving the tractor, Gabriele always dispatched his duties while in mid song.

Mary Clare sent him an iPod jam-packed with the music of the world's greatest classical vocalists. He sang duets with everyone from Pavarotti to Renee Fleming, loving every minute of his in-field concerts, as did his audience of farm workers, passers-by and visitors.

The plantation currently employs one-hundred-fifty people. Its offerings have expanded to include dairy products, fruits and vegetables. The surplus products are sold in restaurants in Nairobi, providing funds for the Diocese's other humanitarian projects.

One day I went with Gabriele as he called on his customers. He looked and acted like an Italian movie star. His customers, mostly female, nearly fainted when they heard him coming, and he could sell them anything. His competitors never stood a chance.

One time a shipping company contacted me at my home in Rochester, inquiring about a missing shipping container used to send medical supplies to Kenya. I knew the container must still be somewhere in Kenya, but I had no idea just where. I found out later that Gabriele had secured the container for his own purposes, placing it on the tea farm where he converted it into a nicely appointed office. The one-time shipping container now had doors and windows, complete with flower pots adorning the sills.

Gabriele and Sarah entering the missing shipping-container-turned-tea farm office.

Father Stephen with workers showing off the tractor Jack provided for the tea farm.

The Woman on the Road

If you are neutral in situations of injustice, you have chosen the side of the oppressor. If an elephant has its foot on the tail of a mouse and you say you are neutral, the mouse will not appreciate your neutrality.

Anglican Bishop Desmond Tutu

In Kenya, cars drive on the left side of the road and are manufactured the same as the cars in England and Japan. The passenger sits on the left and the driver sits on the right.

One day, my friend Sarah Brewin and I were returning to the airport in Nairobi. As we drove along, I saw a woman sitting on the ground beside the road. Her legs were crossed and she had a small charcoal grill in front of her. On her back, secured with a bright cotton cloth folded into a pouch, was a baby. I realized the woman was cooking and selling corn, one ear at a time, to passersby.

As our car approached the woman, our eyes locked and remained so even as the car passed. We travelled a few hundred yards further down the road when I asked the driver to stop and turn around. We made two u-turns, pulling up next to the woman. Stepping out of the car, we leaned down to talk with her. She spoke in broken English, telling us that she had no husband and selling corn was how she supported herself and her baby. Before leaving, I gave her all the Kenyan currency I had left in my pockets.

I often think of that Kenyan woman and her child. I close my eyes and there she is, looking at me with those beautiful eyes, dark and deep. I can't help but think, "Here we are in the United States, the freest and one of the wealthiest countries in the world, and this young mother is probably still back on that street corner eking out a living selling corn on the cob — one ear at a time.

Father George, A Man Who Travels on Faith Alone

One of the priests to come to Rochester from Kenya is Father George Okoth. When Father George first came to the United States, he was living in Williamsburg, Virginia, staying at a home for handicapped adults called Jolly Pond Residential Facility.

Jolly Pond was run by The Little Sisters of St. Francis from Uganda and Kenya. Sister Agnes originally founded Jolly Pond and was in charge of running the facility.

I can not clearly remember how I first met Father George, but it was probably through Sister Agnes.

Father George came to the United States under the assumption that he was granted a scholarship from St. John Fisher College to work toward a master's degree in counseling. However, due to miscommunication, he arrived in Rochester only to learn there was no scholarship in place. To make the situation more challenging, St. John Fisher College didn't even offer a master's degree in counseling at that time.

The Diocese of Rochester allowed Father George to live at the rectory of a poor inner-city parish, but he had no money, no income, and no scholarship.

One day I visited Father at the rectory where he was living. I was surprised to learn that there was practically no food in the house. It was winter, and winter in Rochester can be cold and unforgiving. That day, I found Father George cold, alone, and nearly despondent. He could not believe what was happening to him as he languished in despair.

I took Father George to St. John Fisher College, and things quickly changed for him after we met with Dr. Gerry Rooney, dean of admissions at the college.

Although St. John Fisher College did not offer a master's degree in counseling, Dr. Rooney did some research and suggested that Father George visit the State University of New York College at Brockport, which did offer such a program.

Fortunately, Dr. Rooney knew Brockport's director of graduate admissions, and he called the college and explained the situation. We were given an appointment for the following day.

Now, if you have ever applied for admission to a university to pursue a master's degree, you understand the complexity of the paperwork involved. But we quickly learned that the paperwork was not all that complex if you were on the graduate studies director's fast track. What normally would been months of filling out and filing paperwork was swiftly completed and processed in just hours.

At Brockport, we went from office to office, dean to dean, and by the end of the day George was accepted into the program, assigned his course of study, and had his ID, text books, school jacket, and dining pass in hand. What's more, his entire tuition was paid in full.

Shortly after entering the program at The College at Brockport, Father George was assigned to the wonderful suburban parish named after St. Thomas Moore, where he became close friends with the pastor. Serving at St. Thomas Moore, Father George received a small salary and was provided healthcare insurance. Someone even loaned him a car.

Today Father George is a Captain in the United States Army. He has counseled thousands of young service men and women in peace time and conflict, in the United States and on tours of duty in Iraq, Germany and Afghanistan.

The first time I visited Bungoma, a city in northern Kenya, I traveled with Father George. I was taken aback by the poverty of the people and the dilapidated condition of the city itself. The main street was the primary route through the city for many trucks. Not surprisingly, the blacktop along this busy thoroughfare was long gone. The street, miles long, was worn down to nothing more than a half-round mound of red

My Road to Kenya

clay. On a dry day, a cloud of choking dust would rise from the tires of the passing trucks, settling in a red film on everything, including the people sitting alongside the road selling various items from their stalls. The people of Bungoma, obviously used to the dust, took no notice of the red powder blanketing the city.

My friend and driver, Father George, was driving an old borrowed Datsun at the time. The car had neither springs nor working shock absorbers. Because it also had no air conditioning, we drove through the heat of the day with the windows open.

When we finally stopped for the night, we opened the trunk to retrieve the luggage stored there at the beginning of our trip. I asked Father George if he owned the brown suitecase. He answered no, and said the suitcase was mine. I told him no, my suitcase was not brown, but blue. Reaching over, he brushed some dust from the suitcase. And from beneath a blanket of red road dust my blue suitcase magically appeared. Father George looked at me strangely and said, "Go look in a mirror. Tonight you and I are the same color." And indeed we were.

The entrance to St. Damiano Medical Centre.

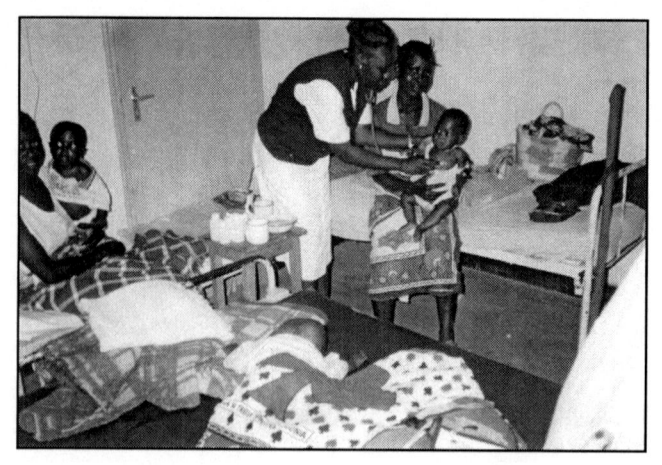

Women caring for children at St. Damiano's.

St. Damiano Hospital, located in Bungoma, is run by The Little Sisters of St. Francis. Father George took me to meet the nuns who owned and managed the hospital, which was too small and under equipped to effectively meet the healthcare needs of their community.

After meeting these women who possess an indomitable spirit, I knew I wanted to build an addition to St. Damiano's. We did so by adding a second floor to the already-existing structure. I later shipped a container of medical equipment and supplies to the hospital, completely re-equipping the facility.

After our visit to St. Damiano's, Father George and I continued on to his home in the Parish of Homa Bay.

In Kenya, the incidence of AIDS is higher in some areas than in others. I did not understand why it was that in some rural areas the HIV/AIDS infection has grown to epidemic proportions. One of these areas lies along the banks of Lake Victoria and includes the city known as Homa Bay.

I inquired about the AIDS epidemic in the area and Father George explained that modern science means nothing to some Kenyans. Many people of Homa Bay believed the source of the illness was from witches who would come to their area and place spells on the people in their village. When local witches were unable to "undo the spells placed on them," it became apparent to many tribesmen that the causes of AIDS were outside the realm of their understanding.

When witchcraft failed to undo the spell and eliminate the disease, the people turned to science for the answers they needed. George reflected, saying, "But by then, for some places, it was just too late."

George also talked about how, in many areas of Kenya, the practice of Wife Inheritance is still quite common. When a man dies in Kenya, his brother is obligated to take the deceased brother's wife and family as his own. This practice includes having conjugal rights with the inherited wife.

When I first learned of Wife Inheritance, my Western sensibilities thought the practice was terrible. But then, upon reflection, I realized that in a country where Social Security is non-existent, family is everything. Brothers commit to care for their brothers' families even in death. The intentions seem noble and logical. As George pointed out, "What woman would not take care of her sister's children and treat them as her own?"

The unintended consequences of Wife Inheritance, however, caused by sexually transmitted disease, has devastated rural families and entire villages practicing these long-held traditions. Many times the brother who had died had already contracted AIDS, passing the HIV virus on to his wife, who in turn would infect her new husband, who again, would infect his original wife or wives.

It is evident the government and religious leaders have made great progress in educating the nation's young people on the causes of HIV/AIDS, which has gone a long way to significantly diminish the number of new cases. But for those who are already infected and without access to medicine, the news comes too late and with tragic and devastating outcomes.

I talked about the importance of offering education and other opportunities to young people in Kenya. Today, the younger, more well-educated are having smaller families. This is helpful in curbing AIDS, as well as providing for a higher standard of living for these young Kenyans. But intervention remains the key to preventing the spread of HIV/AIDS.

For example, when a young girl is denied access to an education, in most cases she will be relegated to a life of poverty. Poverty and hunger are forces that drive many young girls into a life of prostitution, which in turn leads to the transmission of HIV.

It is not uncommon for girls who do not attend secondary school to give birth to one or two children before reaching the age of fifteen or sixteen. For the most part, these young girls are unable to care for themselves and their young children without early and significant intervention. Desperation, disease, hunger, and neglect are all causes leading to premature death for the young people of Kenya. Left behind are the orphans — thousands of orphans — many of whom also are HIV positive or have AIDS. Thus the cycle of poverty begins again, a legacy handed down from generation to generation as children lose their parents, their homes, and any safety net, regardless of how tenuous it might have been.

In Homa Bay, I learned of a small hospital whose staff cared primarily for women and children who suffered from AIDS. A doctor I met there, who was a representative of Doctors without Borders, told me that an estimated fifty percent of the population in the area of Homa Bay was either HIV positive or already suffering from AIDS. He thought that it was the highest density of HIV in the world. I witnessed AIDS for the first time when I toured the hospital, which was run down and overcrowded. Many of the patients were very thin and weak, and were just lying in their beds, not moving. I asked the nurse what was wrong with her patients. At first she mentioned a number of medical problems and then reluctantly explained that most of the patients had AIDS. We agreed that day to build a new hospital in Homa Bay. The new hospital would keep the same name as the old one — St. Paul's Hospital.

Homa Bay sits on the banks of Lake Victoria, which retains much of its natural beauty. But it is difficult, if not impossible, to look beyond the poverty and despair of the people living in the area to see the beauty of the surrounding countryside.

*St. Paul's Hospital stands ready to receive
Homa Bay's sick and suffering.*

We were hosted by Bishop Linus, who was Presiding Bishop of Homa Bay at the time. Linus' quarters consisted of a kitchen, sitting room, and a small bedroom, all of which were filled with books. One thing the home lacked, however, was room for guests. So Father George and I stayed in two small rooms in a motel directly down the street from the Bishop's home.

The first morning of our stay we woke to find there was no hot water for our showers. I complained about this at the motel's front desk. The next morning the problem was solved. We woke to find there was no water at all, which meant there would be no shower, hot or cold, that day.

Father George and Bishop Linus

Homa Bay is Father George's hometown. But, as I mentioned earlier, today he is a Captain in the United States Army. He received his United States citizenship about a decade ago, prior to volunteering as a military chaplain. As I write this, Father George is heading back to Afghanistan for his third tour of duty.

The last time we were together, Father George was visiting us in Rochester. He mentioned that tours in Iraq are more difficult than tours in Afghanistan as temperatures in Iraq often range between 100 and

120 degrees during the day. "The biggest enemy in Iraq is the weather," he told us.

George went on to say that he was looking forward to the cooler weather in Afghanistan, and chuckled when he told us that he would take us on a picnic in the mountains of Afghanistan, if ever we happened to be in the Middle East.

I asked him, "Why do you do what you do?" He said he guessed that being a chaplain was "a calling." He followed up with the thought that when he was a pastor of a small church in the United States, people invited him to share a simple dinner. In war, people asked him for something more — help and advice.

Father George serves between twelve-hundred and thirteen-hundred men and women while on a tour of duty. He spoke of these soldiers as family, telling us that in the military he is a father, friend and advisor to the men and women he serves. "Some men have no family. I become their parent. Whoever I serve is family." Oddly enough, while still in the military, soldiers do not fraternize with one another outside of their tours of duty. "We simply go home or to wherever we are heading next. When soldiers and officers leave the military, they can again talk or meet. It is just the way it is," he said.

At the time of his visit to Rochester, Father George was stationed in Kansas. We were enjoying lunch together at Oak Hill Country Club when Father George's cell phone rang. While he spoke quietly to the party on the other end, we got up and left our table because cell phones are not allowed inside Oak Hill. We moved outside to the veranda where George would be free to talk. I heard him tell his caller that another officer was on duty while he was out-of-town, and that he was returning the following day. He then pulled another phone out of his pocket and dialed a call, alerting the officer on duty that an incoming call was coming his way.

I noted that Father George's long arm was out-stretched as he looked at the buttons on the cell phone. Apparently his eyesight was not what it once was. I kidded him about his graying hair, realizing that we both had aged over the years since we first had become friends. He was no longer the lean, timid young man that I first met over a decade ago.

We continued our conversation and he told me he was heading back to Kansas for a month of training with young soldiers before his deployment. His training would include desert training.

At any age this training is difficult and a tremendous challenge. When I asked him why he chose to take the desert training at his age of fifty-one, he said, "It is a matter of life and death. I will have to be in top physical condition to survive in Afghanistan."

George mentioned that he held great admiration and respect for the privates assigned to guard him. "These soldiers are willing to take a bullet for me," he said, and then specifically mentioned a twenty-one-year-old man who would be traveling with him to Afghanistan. "He is fast, strong and loyal."

As Father George spoke, it was obvious to me that he had great admiration for his guard. I sarcastically kidded Father George, saying, "He'd take a bullet for *you*?" George solemnly nodded in confirmation. I pray that Father George and his guard return home safely.

The phone rang again and the melodious voice of Sister Agnes bellowed over the speaker phone. Laughter ensued as George and Agnes reminisced in Swahili. Sister Agnes chattered at top speed while George apologized that his Swahili skills were somewhat rusty. I jokingly offered to translate, but there were no takers, as I suspect they knew I did not speak a word of the language. Whatever would flow from my lips would merely be disjointed babble created for the purpose of humor. Our shared laughter was a nice way to end the day.

Finding Paradise on Lake Victoria

One of the brightest highlights of all my trips to Kenya came when Father George told me he would like to take me to meet Father Tielen, a Dutch priest who had lived in Kenya for forty years.

Father Tielen lived on the shore of Lake Victoria, about thirty miles north of Homa Bay. George warned me that traveling to Father Tielen's home would not be easy since there were few if any roads between Homa Bay and Father Tielen's home.

Our transportation of choice for the trip was once again the borrowed Datsun with worn-out springs and useless shock absorbers.

Since there was still no air conditioning in the car, we drove with the windows open.

George drove across rough terrain and through deep gullies in a matter-of-fact manner, explaining, "These gullies are not so bad; a big gully is when you have to stop and look down to see if the car ahead of you has fallen in."

Later that day we pulled into a clearing by the shore of Lake Victoria. In front of us stood Father Tielen's self-built house. Large porches and verandas surrounded the house, shading the interior rooms from the heat of the day. Behind the house I could see farm lands stretching down to the lake shore. In front of and across the road from the house was a barracks-like building. As we pulled closer to the house, we found ourselves surrounded by cheering boys of all ages, laughing and racing our car to Father Tielen's house.

Father Tielen and Jack in the background, giving one of Father Tielen's orphaned children a ride in a wheelbarrow.

I learned that Father Tielen had built the house and barracks by hand. I also learned that he cared for two dozen orphans, all of whom had HIV/AIDS. He also planted a four-acre farm to feed himself and the children. Around the circumference of the farm he strung a thin wire fence. The wire stood about four feet off the ground and was held up by wooden poles spaced out to about every ten yards.

I inquired about the fence. Father Tielen explained that at nightfall he attached the wire to a set of car batteries. "When the hippos come out of the lake to eat from my fields, the wire releases a jolt of electricity when they touch it with their noses. It's an effective way of keeping the hippos away from the growing vegetables. Without the wire, the hippos could eat the entire farm in just one night," he said.

Father Tielen was a quiet man who ruled his land with discipline, a firm hand, kindness and compassion. In the barracks lived the twenty-four orphans he cared for with the assistance of one old Kenyan woman who served as cook, housekeeper and nurse to the children. All of the children were HIV positive or already had AIDS.

He told me that he could not worry about the children's health because he had no money for medications for even a few of the boys, never mind all twenty-four. He was a realist, knowing that the best he could do was to give the children as normal a life as possible for as long as possible.

Our days with the children at Lake Victoria were wonderful. Our nights were spent sleeping in hammocks on a veranda no more than sixty feet from the water's edge. Father Tielen assured us that we need not worry about the hippos or the crocodiles living in and around the water, explaining that he had the hippos under control with the electric fence and that the crocs did not venture this far out of the water. He then said, "Sleep well. Have a good night." Feeling reassured, I did just that.

Father Tielen was proud of his farm. The scope and depth of his talents and abilities as a builder, farmer, and father to twenty-four children made me feel like an underachiever. And then I learned that Father Tielen had also built a small church on an island in the middle of Lake Victoria. He built the church so the people living on the island and around the lake would have a place of worship.

Each night at dusk he walked to the distant gazebo, taking with him a few of the boys. They sat together, discussing their day and any personal concerns the boys might have. He explained, "It is the custom in Kenya for a father and his children to meet after dinner for private discussions." Father Tielen, in listening to the boys, was simply taking the place of the children's fathers.

One morning Father Tielen invited us to go on a boat ride with him and the boys. Somehow he had secured an old lifeboat from a cruise ship. It sat twenty-four passengers and still had its oar locks. For power, Father Tielen had removed an engine from a Dodge truck and installed it on the boat, adding a shaft and attaching a propeller. I cannot imagine how he did it. He rigged up a rudder to steer the vessel and had trained his crew of twenty-four how to launch the craft.

Since there was no dock, the boat was launched from shore by rolling it on round logs and pushing it in or pulling it out of the water as required. As soon as he told the boys we were going for a ride, every one of them flew into action, with each one knowing his job. In a matter of minutes, the young crew efficiently launched the boat and we were underway.

On our boat trip we saw groups of men and boys wading and bathing in the lake. In other areas along the shore there were groups of women and young children. The women used the lake to bathe themselves and their children, and to wash their clothes. Mothers, keeping careful watch of their children, allowed them to wade only up to their knees because of the fear of crocodiles. The women and children also kept a modest distance from the men.

My Second Trip to Homa Bay

Of all my experiences in Kenya, one of the most memorable was a trip I took with Father Stephen Mbugua.

We travelled from Stephen's home near Nakuru, heading for Homa Bay. Quite honestly, I do not remember why we were going to Homa Bay for this particular visit, but we must have had a good reason because the trip was long and the travel difficult.

For our accommodations, we were invited to stay in a new building that had been provided for the new Bishop of Homa Bay. Because there was no Bishop serving the area at the time, there were several rooms available at the Bishop's house for visitors to use when in the area. During the day, the building also provided space for offices for various agencies.

We knew in advance finding the building would be difficult. All we knew for certain was that the building was located directly on Lake Victoria and about ten miles from Homa Bay. To top it off, there were no direct roads for getting there. When I say there were no roads, I mean there literally were no roads.

I had been to the Bishop's home before, but was always accompanied by a local guide who knew the way, making sure we traveled only during the light of day.

The directions to the Bishop's house were themselves interesting and went something like this: "Drive out of Homa Bay on the good road, but at a certain point in the road turn left and drive across an open field for about two miles. When you come to a cornfield, take the path that cuts through the corn…"

As you can see, finding the building, even during the best of conditions, took the skills of a trained professional, or at least someone very familiar with that part of the county.

Knowing how difficult it was to find the Bishop's house, Stephen called another priest who said he knew the way and would serve as our driver and guide. The next order of business was to pick up the priest, and so we set out driving. Several hours out of our way from our intended destination of Homa Bay and then the Bishop's house, we finally reached our guide. Unfortunately by then it was already dark.

When night falls in Kenya, it falls into total darkness. To make matters worse, there are no street lights beyond city borders, and in the country there are not even lights shining out from the windows of the houses. In other words, it is just plain pitch dark.

Although the name of the priest who would be driving us was John, Father Stephen always referred to him as simply "That Guy." So I immediately began thinking of Father John as That Guy.

It did not take long before we realized That Guy had no idea how to get to the Bishop's house. We were making our way by a "by-guess and by-golly" means, and we were soon completely lost. But That Guy kept saying, "Don't worry. I know where we are."

Now, to understand the rest of this story you have to know something about Stephen. Stephen has an incredible ability to observe where he is going and where things are in his environment. For instance, he has the uncanny ability to locate a golf ball that has been hit into a stand of trees or thick brush by simply walking right up to it, even if the ball has landed in deep grass. If your golf shots pull or hook, he is your perfect golf partner.

That dark night I was truly thankful for Father Stephen's acute ability of observation, as his hawk-like skill would save us — not just once, but twice — before the night was through.

As we drove through the night with nothing more than the moon and stars to light our way, I heard Father Stephen suddenly scream out in distress, "Stop!" I immediately knew we were in trouble.

Somehow That Guy had managed to drive our car out onto a pier and had Stephen not shouted his warning, our trip would have ended that night in a long fall and cold plunge into Lake Victoria. Sitting in the moonlight, our hearts pounding, we realized we were on the commercial pier in Homa Bay. Driving for more than an hour, we had literally gone nowhere, ending up within one-hundred yards from where we had started. Listening for any creaking of the wooden boards beneath us, we held our breaths as That Guy put the car into reverse and slowly backed us off the pier. When we were once more on solid ground, we set out again for the Bishop's house.

Mbita ferry docked at the wooden pier on Lake Victoria.

We had come perilously close to driving off the pier and into the chill waters of Lake Victoria, and now not even a single ray of light pierced the dark, dark night. I don't think it could have been any darker if we were sitting inside a closet with the lights turned off.

That Guy drove the dark roads and pathways using nothing more than the headlights of oncoming vehicles as his guide, having no idea where in the world he was going.

It wasn't long before Stephen once again yelled "Stop"! That Guy hit the breaks and the car skidded to an abrupt halt. Not knowing where we were, we all climbed out of the car to investigate the situation only to find we were now perched perilously close to the edge of a ravine. Father Stephen wisely took over the driver's seat from that point on.

Well into the night, we finally pulled up to the Bishop's house and waited at the gate for the watchman to come and let us in. But we waited in vain. The Bishop's house, set well back from the entrance to the property, was unoccupied that evening and even the night watchman seemed to be among the missing.

Stephen honked the car horn several times, but no one came to open the gate. Knowing that we were the only guests arriving at the house that night, we realized that the gate would remain closed unless we could find the guard to let us in.

With this in mind, we exited the car and looked around for a way to let ourselves into the compound. It was then that we noticed the night watchman. He was lying in the driveway inside the locked gate. He appeared to be sound asleep, and as we later learned, he was also very much intoxicated.

Being the resourceful person he is, Stephen climbed over the gate, took the keys from the watchman's pocket, and opened the gate himself. Once inside the compound, we pulled the watchman out of the driveway and dragged him into the gate house. We placed the sleeping man in an upright position in one of the gatehouse chairs.

As if the seat of the chair had been greased, the unconscious watchman immediately slipped from the chair, landing in a heap on the floor. I decided it wouldn't be right for us to leave the man on the floor, so we once again picked him up and placed him back in his chair.

With great speed and grace the watchman once again slid to the floor and lay there in his deep, intoxicated sleep. Father Stephen and I looked at each other, shrugged, then turned and left the gatehouse. Shutting the door behind us, we left the watchman to sleep in peace.

Once we were settled inside the Bishop's house, Father Stephen, who takes great pleasure in making jokes, tried to convince That Guy and me that there was a good chance bandits would raid the house that night. Since there was no watchman on duty or even awake, his story resonated with both of us. He went on, telling us that the good Fathers — Stephen and That Guy — would sleep upstairs and I was to be the lone man relegated to spending the night sleeping in a room on the ground floor and closest to the building's front door.

I couldn't let Father Stephen get away with his joke at my expense. I removed the cardboards from my dry-cleaned shirts and used them to make signs for any intruders who might enter the premises that evening. In large bold letters I wrote, "The rich guys with the money are sleeping upstairs." I strategically placed the signs on the front door and at the foot of the stairs. And then I went to sleep.

Cloistered Nuns Throw a Curve Ball

My usual routine upon arriving in Kenya was to stay a few days with Archbishop Ndingi. As the Archbishop left for work each day, I would settle myself on his front porch to read whatever I had on hand at the time. One day I decided instead of reading I would take a walk through the neighborhood, which I always found quite interesting. After a short distance, I noticed a building that looked like an old monastery. As it turned out, the building was actually a cloistered convent for Carmelite nuns.

I did not know this when I entered the building. I let myself into the convent's reception area and, finding no one there, I took a look around. Noticing a buzzer on the far wall, I walked over and pressed it. Almost immediately a pleasant voice was speaking to me from the intercom, asking, "Who is there"? I recognized the voice as that of a woman's, and assuming it was one of the nuns, I told her I was a guest of the Archbishop out for a walk. The next thing she asked me was,

"Are you American?" "Yes," I replied. She quickly said, "We will be right there."

A moment later, two smiling, round-faced Carmelite nuns entered the room. Both wore glasses and appeared to be in their seventies. On their heads they wore headpieces known as wimples. Their bodies were draped from head to toe in neatly pressed white habits. Each wore a long, plain rosary around her waist.

One of the sisters, appearing to be a Superior, inquired, "Can we ask you a question?" "Sure," I said. I don't know what I expected them to ask me, but what they said next wasn't it. "Do you follow baseball," she questioned. "Yes," I answered. "How are the Cleveland Indians doing," she asked. Before I could say, the other nun asked, "What about the Pittsburgh Pirates?"

Egerton University

Egerton University, located in Nakuru, was founded in 1939 as a school of agriculture. Its mission at the time was to prepare European youths for careers in farming. Lord Maurice Egerton of Tatton established the school through a seven-hundred-forty-acre land grant. In 1958, Lord Egerton donated another eleven-hundred acres for the school. Shortly thereafter the school opened its doors to students of all races. Since its early days, Egerton has grown to include three campuses and two constituent schools. Today, Egerton University is a public university, which prepares students to become nurses, doctors, teachers, farmers, business men and women, and more. Students of all ethnicities and religions from around the globe are welcome to study at Egerton.

The main purpose for one of my visits to Kenya was to attend the grand opening of a building newly constructed next to Egerton University. How I ended up getting involved in this venture to begin with had to do with a friend named Bishop Peter Nyeri.

Some years before, Bishop Nyeri, a St. John Fisher College graduate and then Bishop of Nakuru, began construction of a building adjacent to the Egerton University campus. The Bishop wanted a facility that would serve as a social and religious meeting place for faculty, students and friends. Shortly after construction had begun funds ran out and the building sat unfinished for quite some time. But Bishop Nyeri's dream of having a gathering place remained strong.

Through Father Stephen, again in the role of general contractor, Bishop Nyeri asked if I would provide the funds needed to finish the building. I readily agreed. The completed building included space for a variety of offices, a four-classroom nursery school and a tailoring school, as well as a small clinic and community hall for seminars and workshops.

Edgerton University student center and nursery school, named St. Augustine's Chaplaincy Hall, is shown to the left of St. Augustine Church.

Nursery school children at St. Augustine's Chaplaincy Hall.

Grand opening ceremonies at St. Augustine's Chaplaincy Hall with Jack, far left, and President Daniel Moi seated beside him.

On opening day of the new building, the recently "retired" president of Kenya, Daniel Moi, attended the ceremonies. He arrived with a small entourage of Humvees and bodyguards armed with automatic rifles. This all seemed extremely out of place — Kenya's most powerful dictator with armed guards attending a ceremony opening a new building at a university. But, when President Moi learned of the building project, he insisted on making the facility larger than planned and donated money to the project. Many others also gave of their time, talents, and resources to see the project through.

Among other things, President Moi was especially noted for his longevity of rule. He was originally elected president for one four-year term but had managed through various means to remain in power for more than twenty years — sometimes with elections taking place giving him the privilege to remain in office and sometimes without.

Throughout its recent history, many elections in Kenya have been riddled with corruption which led to tribal and civil unrest. Whenever this happened, the "official" government would declare martial law, cancelling the elections, and thus remaining in power.

One of the more unusual ways Moi successfully secured control over the balloting was to eliminate the one-step private-voting process. Instead of using secret ballots, eligible voters participating in the country's elections were required to indicate their choices in an open two-step electoral process known as queue-voting.

The first step involved voters standing in a line with other voters at the polling places, openly declaring their support for their candidate of choice. As the party in power, Moi's party line was deemed the politically correct line of choice. The immensely brave voters standing in queues for candidates other than Moi could be easily recognized and their choice of candidate noted, with possible dire consequences to them or their families.

The second step of the process was for provincial administrators to count the number of people in line behind each candidate. Obviously, the line or lines containing the greatest number of people signified the winner of each provincial or national election.

During the ceremonies marking the opening of the school, I joked several times, whispering to Stephen to ask President Moi to give me back the $50 visa surcharge I had been obliged to pay upon entering the country. The fee levied at the airport was collected in cash and was believed to be deposited into Moi's personal accounts. But Stephen discouraged me from saying anything because challenging Kenya's leader over a $50 charge would most likely have been detrimental to my health.

When the ceremony was over, President Moi graciously invited Father Stephen and I to join him for tea the next day. Unfortunately, we declined the opportunity because we already had plans to leave the area. In retrospect, I wish we had accepted President Moi's invitation. Visiting his home, which lies within the confines of an army barracks, would have been an interesting experience.

I.M.E.C.
An Angel of Mercy

There were also many opportunities for us to re-equip existing hospitals, and did so through a company in North Andover, Massachusetts called International Medical Equipment Cooperative (I.M.E.C.).

I.M.E.C. collects and refurbishes used medical equipment, shipping it to hospitals around the world. In all, we contracted with them to refurbish about fifteen hospitals throughout Kenya.

I.M.E.C. was founded by Tom Keefe, who decided to do something about the waste of medical equipment he saw in American hospitals. He has made it his mission to ensure that valuable and even life-saving equipment is saved, collected, refurbished and delivered to hospitals and clinics around the world.

I.M.E.C. primarily collects equipment from hospitals and other healthcare facilities throughout the northeastern United States, and transports it to its two-hundred-fifty-thousand-square-foot refurbishing shop and warehouse, where the equipment is reconditioned to look and work as it did when it was new. It is then packaged, not as individual pieces of equipment, but in what is categorized as a "suite." A suite could include everything needed for a fully functioning operating room, dental department, medical library, birthing center, or even a waiting room. In all, I.M.E.C. inventories more than sixty types of suites for just about every kind of room or facility a hospital might require.

Tom requires the equipment and supplies sent overseas to be in excellent condition and in good working order. Detail-oriented and particular about the quality and appearance of everything I.M.E.C. provides, he believes sending a product that does not meet his standards is an insult to the people on the receiving end. In referring to his customers, he once said to me, "They do not have very much to start with, so I am not going to insult them by sending containers of supplies and equipment that are not of high quality."

The process of shipping a suite begins when an individual or organization referred to as a "shepherd" brings a proposed project to I.M.E.C. for consideration. Once I.M.E.C. receives the proposal, a volunteer doctor working on behalf of I.M.E.C. will typically make a preliminary visit to the medical facility making the request. The doctor makes a thorough inspection of the premises and ascertains the needs and viability of the site as sustainable for refurbishing.

If the I.M.E.C. representative determines that the clinic or hospital is a candidate for refurbishment, the doctor then creates a needs-assessment list and floor plan of the building. Back at I.M.E.C.'s facility in North Andover, a detailed inventory of all the equipment to be sent to the hospital is prepared and actually incorporated into the floor plan. In my case, Dr. Susan Crawford acted as the I.M.E.C. volunteer assessing the hospitals we hoped to refurbish in Kenya.

Once all the preliminary inspections and assessments were made and the sites designated viable, the various requested suites would be packed on skids, loaded into forty-foot containers, and shipped to Kenya. The equipment, arriving at the port of Mombasa on the Indian Ocean, would be transferred by train to Embakasi near Nairobi, a clearing and customs depot for containers entering Kenya.

The shepherd is required to make arrangements for a clearing agent and trucks to meet the containers, receive the goods, and then deliver them to a particular hospital.

At first the collection, shipping, and distribution of medical supplies and equipment seemed like a very complicated process. If not done properly, the paperwork required for exporting and importing medical products, threatened to delay shipments. Each document had to be meticulously completed or containers would languish at the port of entry. Delays would lead to expensive storage fees and costly supplemental charges. This was the scenario we faced in the early days of our work shipping goods to Kenya.

Besides the help of Dr. Crawford, I was fortunate to work with Sarah Brewin, RN, who arranged to receive the containers once they arrived in Embakasi and ensured their delivery to the recipient hospital's door. After a few missed cues, we learned how to receive the containers in Kenya with very few problems.

For a number of years, partnering with I.M.E.C. to refurbish hospitals became our largest single activity in Kenya. It made more sense to re-equip existing hospitals than to build new ones. In each case, the hospital was visited before the equipment was shipped and after it was received by the hospital. Dr. Crawford is the one who always revisited the facility for our projects, ensuring that the equipment had arrived and was working properly.

The financial arrangements between I.M.E.C. and my group were simple. I.M.E.C. would place a value on the equipment being shipped based on the selling price of used medical equipment in the United States. The value of used medical equipment was about one tenth of that of new equipment. Pricing things in this manner meant that a typical container consisted of somewhere between $300,000 and $400,000 worth of medical equipment. The value of this used medical equipment, if new, would have been in the millions of dollars.

I.M.E.C. charged the shepherd only a fraction of the container's value. Typically a container would cost a shepherd $15,000 to $25,000. This fee enabled I.M.E.C., a not-for-profit organization staffed primarily by volunteers, to pay their few employees and the expenses for gathering and refurbishing the equipment.

The frugal management style of this organization is a model for any not-for-profit. For example, Wednesday is the main day that volunteers work in the warehouse. On each Wednesday, Tom Keefe's mother cooks lunch for all the volunteers who come to work on the equipment. This is what is called keeping down the cost of overhead.

In addition to purchasing the equipment, the shepherd pays for the cost of shipping the container. Shipping our containers to Kenya cost approximately $5,000 for each one.

Often I.M.E.C. secured free shipping for our containers through a United States government agency that funded shipping containers containing humanitarian supplies. There were also costs for the delivery of the containers from Mombasa to the hospitals, as well as the import duties levied by the Kenyan government. Usually these additional costs amounted to another $5,000. Essentially one could ship $400,000 worth of medical equipment from North Andover, Massachusetts to a small town in Kenya for about $35,000. To me, it was one of the great bargains available in fulfilling charity projects.

Chapter 3
Giving Our Best

Basic Care Brings Health and Hope

As your faith is strengthened, you will find that there is no longer the need to have a sense of control. Things will flow as they will.

E. Teney

Each project we worked on in Kenya was unique. However, some of these projects stand out in my memory more than others.

Father Anthony Ndungo, Archbishop Ndingi's long-time secretary, asked Sarah Brewin and me to visit Saint Bakhita's, a new clinic outside of Nairobi built by an order of Catholic nuns.

Father Anthony wanted to know if we could equip the clinic.

Sarah and I were met at the clinic by Sister Mary Brenda, a nun from South Bend, Indiana, charged with building and managing the facility. We discovered that Father Anthony had not clearly communicated to Sister Mary Brenda the reason for our visit, and it was only when we had almost completed the inspection that she understood.

Sarah and I were surprised upon entering the clinic to find that the facility was brand new. It was also completely empty except for one, solitary chair.

We moved from room to room taking pictures and making notes. Near the end of our tour Sister Mary asked quizzically, "Could you

My Road to Kenya

please explain what you two are doing here?" Sarah, in her typical straightforward manner, responded, "We are going to furnish and equip this whole clinic for you."

A most astonished look crossed Sister Mary's face. Folding her hands together, she began to pray. Finally, raising her eyes to meet ours, she asked, "Do you really mean it"?

Sarah and Sister Mary Brenda became great friends, and Sarah took special care in helping to equip the building. She even carried to Kenya rolls of window screening she purchased in the United States. The screens would be used to cover all the windows in the building to keep out the mosquitoes. As I think back, I do not remember ever seeing any other building in Kenya with window screens.

Utawala, Kenya – Installation visit May 2007

Library

Exam Room

Tea room

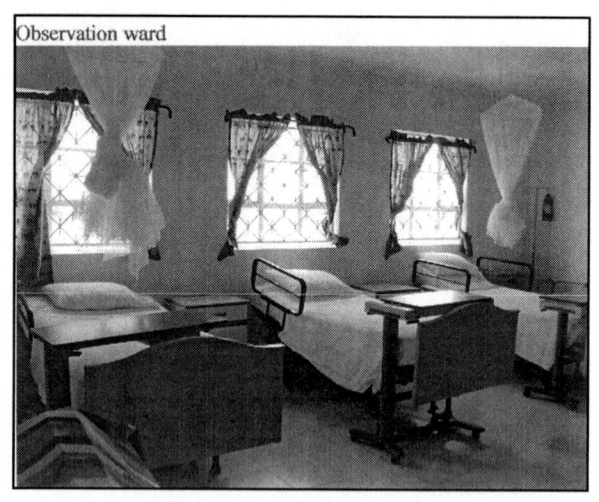

St. Bakita's ward awaits its first patients.

The Slums of Nairobi

The largest project we worked on in Kenya was the delivery of medical equipment and supplies to Ruaraka Uhai Neema Hospital, an integrated medical institution located on the edge of the slums of Nairobi. One side of the hospital overlooks the Moi International Sport Center and the famous Five Star Safari Hotel. Close by are the pitiful slums for which the city is also known. It is estimated that more than one-million people live in these slums.

You may recall the slum scenes in the motion picture *The Constant Gardner*. Those scenes were filmed on location in this area of Nairobi.

One must see the slum for themself to believe such a place even exists on this earth. The community is built primarily of cardboard and sheet metal huts void of electricity or sanitation.

More fortunate residents have access to small rations of kerosene and wood for a creating a fire for heat and cooking or some meager light at night.

Some residents have blankets and warm clothing to fight off the chill night air; however, many residents are not as fortunate. Most adults and children live in cold, cruel, abject poverty and squalor in this forgotten corner of the world. Hunger, abuse, disease and violence are prevalent. And when it rains, life becomes even more unbearable. It is not uncommon to see children barefooted and wading in mud, while feces float on the water collecting in pools in the streets.

The Catholic Diocese of Nairobi donated land to a group of Italian organizations and a charity known as World Friends to build a large healthcare institution to serve the slum's residents. Rafael Ndingi, Bishop at the time, sent Father Antony to visit me in Rochester. The year was 2007. He carried with him the plans for the Neema Center. Father Antony's goal was to find a way to equip the center after it was built.

Building Neema Hospital

Father Antony arrived with detailed plans in hand. After he showed me a list of needed medical equipment and supplies, we headed to I.M.E.C. to visit with Tom Keefe. Upon hearing our project presentation and without a moment's hesitation, Tom said, "We'll do it."

Dr. Crawford was dispatched to visit the hospital, inspect the facilities and meet with hospital officials and doctors. One of the unique requirements for this particular hospital was a burn center. In the overcrowded slums, fires caused by careless residents cooking or seeking warmth from their open fires are common. Burns and smoke inhalation are a major cause of death among residents and, as usual, it is the children who suffer the most.

The prevalent cause of suffering and death for children injured in fires is not so much burns as it is inhaled smoke. Smoke from a fire creates soot, coating the lining of the children's lungs, making it difficult for them to breathe.

The function of the burn unit was not only to treat burns, but to restore breathing for those whose lungs had become coated with soot.

Upon her return from her initial observation visit, Dr. Crawford took great care in acquiring equipment and supplies for the hospital. Special equipment for flushing soot from the lungs of smoke victims were procured and shipped, and any items not in stock at I.M.E.C. were purchased.

Jack W. O'Leary & Mary Clare Lyons with Virginia Elizabeth Rose

Suites of medical equipment are made ready for shipping to Neema Hospital. They include suites for critical care, special care, special procedures, and others.

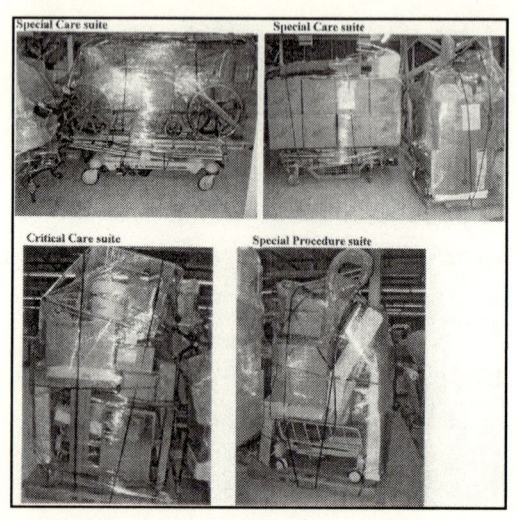

Additional hospital suites await transport to Neema Hospital.

My Road to Kenya

Unloading shipments of medical equipment at their destination at Neema Hospital 2008.

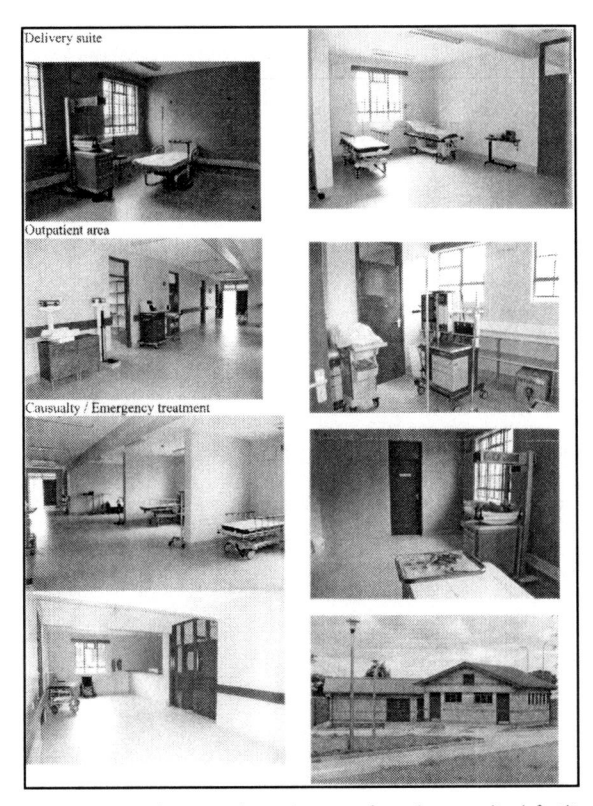

Neema Hospital is transformed into a first-class medical facility.

Neema Hospital is an integrated healthcare institution for the people living in the slums of Nairobi, Kenya.

Neema Hospital became fully operational in March 2009. Under the guidance of Italian and Kenyan doctors, the hospital is growing and expanding its services. Believe it or not, our Italian tenor/tea-farmer/accountant Gabriele holds the position of chief financial officer at the hospital. Recently, Gabriele informed me that Neema Hospital serves four-hundred patients a day, or more than one-hundred-forty-thousand people per year.

Intervol to the Rescue

During renovation of the various hospitals, a secondary need soon became apparent. Consumable medical supplies, such as surgical instruments, bandages, gloves, masks, and so on were identified and I.M.E.C. stepped in to help, providing these much-needed items for each of the suites they shipped.

Eventually these original supplies were exhausted by the hospitals and needed replenishing. Fortunately, we found an organization in Rochester named Intervol to supplement I.M.E.C.'s shipments.

Intervol is run by Dr. Ralph Pennino and Dr. Timothy O'Connor, who, besides being full-time plastic surgeons, run and operate Intervol. Dr. Ralph and Dr. Tim make their way to Belize on an annual basis, providing their medical services to the children there. Dr. Pennino priorities, besides family, are: 1) caring for children in third-world countries, 2) collecting medical supplies for third-world countries, 3) his medical practice, and 4) Notre Dame football — perhaps not in that particular order.

Typically, in an American hospital, a kit of surgical supplies for an operation is sent into the operating room in advance. A surgical kit contains many items. If a surgeon needs only some of the items in the kit for a particular procedure, the unused items are routinely discarded.

Dr. Pennino developed a process that trains hospital staff in the Rochester area to not discard unused medical supplies, but instead to put them in Intervol containers that he provides, which are then picked up and taken to a warehouse where the goods are sorted, boxed, and then distributed to healthcare facilities in developing countries.

When I first worked with Intervol, Doug Castner managed the warehouse. He was instrumental in helping me understand the process of shipping medical supplies. At that time, he was a one-man show. Our containers were initially shipped to Archbishop Ndingi's house, stored in area garages and then distributed to the hospitals.

This process was not ideal, so Sarah Brewin went to Kenya and found a warehouse for us to lease. We hired two employees, purchased forty used computers from Rochester General Hospital, and shipped the computers to the warehouse in Kenya. Sarah distributed the computers to forty different hospitals to be used for ordering needed supplies directly from our warehouse via the Internet. The available inventory would be displayed on the system, allowing hospitals to check to see if the supplies they needed were in stock. The warehouse notified the hospital when the order was ready for pickup.

Sarah Brewin deserves all the credit for implementing this system, and Dr. Ralph Pennino and his team deserve all the credit for making the medical supplies available.

Using an arrangement similar to the one we developed with I.M.E.C., we purchased the containers of supplies from Intervol at a low price and shipped them to Kenya. Occasionally we found organizations willing to pay the costs for shipping the supplies to the Port of Mombasa.

We sent more than thirty shipping containers filled with supplies to our warehouse. Soon we were providing medical supplies to eighty healthcare facilities in and around Nairobi.

Intensive care unit beds, anesthesia machines, delivery beds, isolates for newborns, and many, many other items were given to these facilities. Their only "fee" was that they had to pick up their medical supplies and equipment at the warehouse.

The Warehouse and Distribution Center stocked with medical supplies.

The anesthesia machines were an interesting find. I learned from Doug Castner that Rochester General Hospital was replacing twenty anesthesia machines; a multimillion-dollar endeavor. I made an offer to purchase the used machines through Doug. The offer was accepted and Doug transported the machines to Intervol and then packed each one individually and placed them in a forty-foot container. He then shipped them to our warehouse in Kenya, where we learned they could not be utilized because the Kenyan hospitals used a different type of anesthesia gas than what is routinely used in the United States.

Sarah Brewin did a great deal of research, but none of the fixes or proposed solutions for making the machines operational worked. Shortly thereafter, Sarah met a nurse in Kenya who claimed she could make the machines work. Sarah asked the nurse to create a list of the parts she believed were needed.

We had tried several avenues to re-equip the machines without success and were a bit discouraged as well as skeptical as to whether this new fix would actually work. Nonetheless, the parts were ordered in the United States and delivered to the warehouse in Kenya. As soon as the parts arrived, the nurse went to work on one of the machines. To our surprise and delight she was able to do what she promised. Her modifications to the machine worked.

After hearing the good news about the first machine, we bought nineteen additional sets of parts and all nineteen machines were converted to meet Kenyan specifications. Five years later, all twenty machines are still working in twelve different hospitals.

Sarah Brewin and Sister Mary took their collaboration yet another step farther. They held two healthcare conferences attended by more than four-hundred healthcare professionals.

Chapter 4
No One Left Behind

Building Homes for Children and the Disabled
Children are the hands by which we take hold of heaven.
H.W. Beecher

As I mentioned earlier, Father George Akoth is currently a chaplain and a Captain in the United States Army. He has served tours of duty in Iraq and Germany and is currently deployed in Afghanistan.

Some years ago, when I was traveling with him in Kenya, we visited another Kenyan priest, Father Protus Hamisi. Father Protus is a friend who also attended St. John Fisher College and had become pastor in a new church in northern Kenya near the Ugandan border.

When we arrived at Father Protus's church, we found that he lived in a modest home on the parish grounds. An old church, too small to accommodate the number of parishioners who attended weekly services, stood nearby. Instead of being used as a house of worship, the church was now a storehouse for corn harvested from parish fields.

During our visit, Father Protus took us to an old building that must have been a barn at one time. The old converted barn had been turned into a house for handicapped children. The building was empty except for straw mattresses on the floor. This is where the children slept. I asked Father Protus, "Where do these children come from"? He explained that people began dropping off the handicapped children shortly after he started the parish. They would just leave them there and go on their way. The only place he had for the children to live was in the barn.

To help with the chores that accompany a barn filled with handicapped children, Father Protus hired a young girl of just sixteen to cook and clean. He explained that they managed on a very limited diet, consisting primarily of ground corn boiled in a large black pot outdoors over an open fire.

Upon returning to the United States, we sent Father Protus a shipping container filled with beds, mattresses, bedding and other supplies.

The young girl and the children remained on my mind for a long time. I wanted to build them a better home. One day while I was in the locker room at Oak Hill, my friend Jim Ryan, Sr. asked me what I was currently doing in Africa. I explained that I wanted to build a home for some handicapped children.

He thought for a minute then asked what it would cost to build such a facility. I told him approximately what I thought it would cost, and he said, "I will make you a deal. I will pay for half of it, if we dedicate the home to Sarah Ryan." Sarah was Jim's daughter-in-law who passed away at the age of 35 years old, and he wanted to honor her memory. I agreed to his proposal and we sealed the deal. Together we would build the children their new home.

Once construction began, Jim's entire family became involved in the project. His daughters Megan Minges and Maura Kelly wrote about the project to their family and friends, particularly Sarah Ryan's friends. We received many cash donations as a result of these letters, enabling us to build an even larger home than we first envisioned and with more amenities.

I never met Sarah Ryan, but judging from the numerous letters sent with the contributions from her many friends, she must have been a special person. In addition to the donations received from the Ryans' friends and family, we also received a grant from the Dorothea Haus Ross Foundation in Rochester, which enabled us to complete the project.

When the house was finished, Father Protus planned a grand opening, and a group of us involved in the project traveled to Kenya for the ceremonies. The group consisted of Jim Ryan Sr., Jim Ryan Jr., Maura Minges, Megan Kelly, Mary Clare Lyons, Sister Mary Brenda, Sarah Brewin, and a newcomer named John Anderson, who called me a few weeks before we left for Kenya and asked if he could join us. Thank God he did.

It was snowing when we congregated at the airport in Rochester to begin our journey, and soon all the flights were cancelled. Before long the airport was closed. Other airports on the East coast also were closing one by one, and it looked as if we were going to be stranded even before we began our trip. It was a Wednesday and we wanted to land in Nairobi on Thursday night to enjoy a two-day drive to Eldoret.

Sizing up the situation, John Anderson pulled out his Blackberry and plotted a new course to Kenya.

We stood near the front of the line at the Northwest Airlines ticket counter with hundreds of other frustrated flyers lined up behind us.

Originally scheduled to fly from Rochester to Detroit, then on to Amsterdam and finally Nairobi, our group realized this itinerary would no longer work.

When John finally arrived at the front of the line, he suggested a new route to the airline attendant. First, we would drive to Hamilton, Ontario in Canada and from there we would fly to Montreal on Canadian Airlines. From Montreal, we would fly Swiss Air to Zurich, Switzerland and from there to Nairobi, Kenya. He explained, "We would be a day late, but we could still get there in time for the dedication of the children's home."

The ticket agent at first said, "This is impossible. We cannot book you on other airlines. You have to fly on later flights with Northwest even though it might be days from now." Watching the ticket agent look down the line of more than one-hundred people trying to rebook their own cancelled flights on Northwest, John said to him, "You can get rid of six people at one time, if you agree to this request." The agent ticketed us via John's itinerary.

John arranged for a limousine to pick us up the next morning at fifteen-minute intervals, starting at three o'clock. One by one we were collected by the car that would drive us to Hamilton, Ontario for the first leg of the trip.

By morning, deep drifts of snow made it a struggle for some of us to get from our doors to the waiting car at the end of the driveway. It was so cold inside the limousine on our drive to Hamilton that ice formed on the inside and outside of the car windows. Using the warmth of my hand, I tried to melt the ice on the window on my side of the car to improve visibility as we drove along, but to no avail. My hand just froze to the window glass. In spite of the long, cold car trip, John's plan worked and, through a series of flight hoppings, we arrived in Kenya and only a day behind our original schedule.

We arrived on Friday night, not Thursday as planned, which meant that instead of having two days to drive from Nairobi to Eldoret where the home was located, we had only one day to make the two-day drive. A few hours into the drive, John asked, "Jack, did you know the drive was going to be this difficult?" I said, "I knew this was going to be difficult, especially in some places where there are no roads. But if we were to fly to Eldoret instead of driving this leg of our trip, you wouldn't have gotten the opportunity to see the real Kenya."

Later that day John agreed; all the inconvenience of the difficult car trip was worth the incredible experience of driving the roads through Kenya. Where else can you look out the window of your car and experience the panoramic views of the Great Rift Valley?

Our drive took us past Lake Bagoria where hundreds of thousands of pink flamingos stood feasting on algae from the lake's saline-rich waters. We watched wandering zebras and graceful giraffes as we carved our path toward our initial stop in Nakuru. We passed through patchwork villages and travelled down roads where vendors dressed in colorful garb sat by the roadside selling their goods. We saw boys and girls running, laughing and playing games near their village homes, while others begged for a few Kenyan shillings from passers-by to buy food.

Aside from the amazing wildlife, one of the most unique features of the drive and something that you would not see in the United

States was the site of workers laying forty miles of water pipe by hand. The workers used no tools other than shovels and pickaxes to dig the trenches because the cost of manual labor was much less than the cost of using mechanized digging equipment.

The small bus we rented for the trip sat ten or twelve people. By then we numbered nine in all. Maura, Megan and Mary Clare sat together in the back seat totally absorbed in their conversation. We tried to interrupt by saying things like, "Look, a herd of elephants" or "That volcano just erupted," but nothing swayed them from their chatting. Deep in their own conversation, they were seemingly oblivious to the rest of the world.

Arriving at our hotel in Eldoret, we rolled out of the car and headed for the hotel's tavern for something to quench our thirst after the day's long drive. It was a Saturday night and we were staying in a hotel with rooms above a discotheque. The pounding of the music and the noise from the bar and dance floor kept some of us awake for most of the night.

I woke up the next day a bit weary and restless, and made my way to the dining room where I joined the others for a wonderful English-style Sunday breakfast.

After a few cups of coffee and some toast, eggs, and baked tomatoes, we drove to the town of Soy to visit the newly completed home for handicapped children.

After touring the new building, we went outside for the opening Mass and celebration. Father Hamisi estimated that two-thousand people had come to join in the festivities. We enjoyed more than three hours of singing, dancing and celebration, and witnessed great joy.

Later, John, Jim Ryan, Sr. and I visited Father Protus at his house. Together we came to the decision that the children's home needed three enhancements: a separate kitchen to replace the current open-fire kitchen, a deeper well to increase the water supply, and a laundry for washing clothes. It was fortunate we did. The following year, one-thousand refugees came to live on the parish grounds, and the additions were instrumental in sustaining their daily lives.

My Road to Kenya

The newly built home for disabled children in Soy, Kenya.

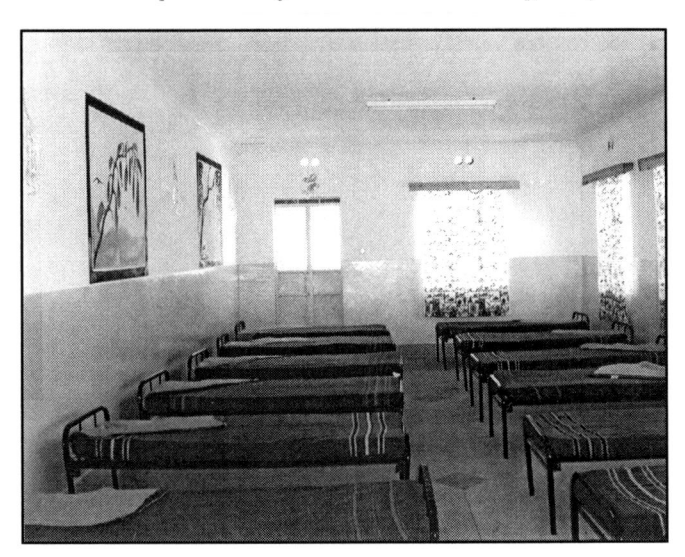

The boy's dormitory at the Sarah Vanderveer Ryan home for disabled children.

Jack W. O'Leary & Mary Clare Lyons with Virginia Elizabeth Rose

The home for disabled children was dedicated
"In loving memory of Sarah Vanderveer Ryan."
"May only smiles, hope, and love penetrate these walls."

My Road to Kenya

The community joined in giving thanks, celebrating the opening of the children's home. Top: Mary Clare Lyons is surrounded by curious children who wanted to confirm for themselves that, indeed, her eyes were blue. Bottom left: A luncheon is served, following the celebration mass. Bottom right: Jack O'Leary and Jim Ryan help with a tree planting.

On Safari

With the celebration of the home and the children who lived there becoming a cherished memory, we went on safari to Masai Mara, one of the most famous game preserves in Africa.

The vast plains of Masai Mara are home to the world's greatest collection of wildlife. Sightings of antelope, gazelle, zebra, giraffe, hippos, and numerous species of birds are common. The goal of a first-time safari participant is to view the "Big Five," which include lions, leopards, elephants, rhinos and buffalo.

Almost everyone has seen the famous films of the wildebeest crossing the Mara River as crocodiles watch and wait for just the right moment to strike.

The migration of animals is a complex and continuous process in East Africa and not every safari participant is fortunate enough to view all or even any of the vast variety of animals — both prey and predator.

Wildebeest, for example, travel in large herds over an area of eighteen-hundred miles. When the grazing of the herds and hot sun exhaust water sources and grazing lands in one area, the herds migrate to another. Depending on climate conditions, the animals, using their acute sense of smell, follow their noses to areas where food and water are more plentiful.

The hungry nomads are in constant motion, making their way across the land, closely followed by the predators that lay in wait. By the time they hit the Mara Plains, the migrating herds number an estimated five-hundred-thousand strong.

A typical day at the game preserve started at 5:30 a.m. for our group. Each morning we would gather for breakfast at first light then pile into two safari cars with open roofs that allowed us to stand up for a better view of the animals.

All the cars returned to the compound at about 11 a.m. for a lunch break and mid-day rest. At 4 p.m., the cars went out again for the second trip of the day.

An unbendable rule on safari is that all cars must be back in the compound by 6:15 p.m., just before the dark of night sets in. If any safari car is not back at the compound by 6:30, the guards contact the car by radio to confirm that everything is alright and that the car will soon return. It is extremely difficult to find the way back to the compound in the dark since there are virtually no roads within the preserve.

Sarah Brewin has enjoyed staying at many of the lodges in the park. Her favorite is the Mara Serena Lodge because of its exquisite accommodations, panoramic views, and location on a hill high within the park. The lodge area, from its hilltop vantage point, provides breathtaking views and an unobstructed panorama of the plains, and the giraffes and elephants crossing in the distance.

The grounds are surrounded by a fence and thick hedges to keep animals outside of the compound. The smaller lodges where we slept are scattered at the bottom of the hill below the main lodge.

Carefully placed along the paths throughout the compound were a number of wooden posts, each with a red emergency button centered on top. The paths connecting the sleeping quarters with each other and the main lodge were dimly lit at night, and, even with the red lights on top of the posts, it was difficult to find one's way around in the dark. A small red-and-white sign nailed to each post read, "Press emergency button to alert guards if wild life is spotted on premises."

I pondered what it would be like to encounter a wild animal on the premises, in the dark of night, on a path with barely enough light to see where you were and where you were headed.

Jim Ryan, Jr. is a serious runner and exercise fanatic. Feeling a bit closed in by the gates, he asked if there was somewhere he could go for a run. The guard looked at him and answered, "It all depends on how fast you can run," and went on to say, "Hyenas can chew through your bones in one bite." We learned that hyenas are the most dangerous animals in the park, especially at night. I recalled seeing the reflective eyes of the hyenas hiding in the bushes as we entered the park the day before. On one of his runs within the park, a family of wort hogs crossed the path just in front of Jim. Neither paid any heed to one another.

As the sun set on our second day of safari, feeling mellow and satisfied with our day, we went into the lodge for dinner. Serving ourselves from the buffet, we retired to a large table where we enjoyed delicious food and congenial conversation for the remainder of the evening.

One day Jim Ryan, Sr. did not feel well, so instead of joining us on safari he stayed in camp where he settled in a comfortable spot, with book in hand, spending his day studying the habits of the animals that live on the Serengeti.

Putting the rest of his time to more good use, he prepared a questionnaire that would test our understanding of the native wildlife. Jim's series of questions primarily focused on the mating habits of the local animal species. I will not repeat all of the questions or the outrageous answers that we provided. Let's just say that his questions focused on items such as the reproductive habits of lions and giraffes and other Masai Mara inhabitants. Even the answers to questions like, "How does the male giraffe know that the female giraffe is agreeable?" and "How long is an average elephant's trunk?" were answered all in good fun.

Some answers to the questions were so absurd that some of us wondered why Jim never wavered from his question sheet. One of the group's females had some particularly humorous and outrageous answers, and I thought that Jim might be offended by her remarks, but she said, "Don't worry, he can't hear all the answers; his hearing aid is turned off." Laughter and relief ensued.

The following morning we saw an injured lion and water buffalo. The warden suspected the two had engaged in a battle for their lives; both appeared weak and mortally wounded. With their energy spent and no longer able to fight, the wounded warriors retreated into the brush where they lay about one-hundred yards apart. Our safari driver explained they would most likely be killed by other predators before nightfall.

Later that day our safari vehicle began to wobble, and it was clear the driver was having difficulty maintaining control. As luck would have it, our vehicle had a flat tire.

My Road to Kenya

Despite previous warnings to always stay in our vehicle, we were asked to get out of the truck so our driver could jack-up the vehicle for the necessary tire change. We exited with some trepidation but, as good fortune would have it, we could not detect any wildlife in the area. We nervously took turns photographing each other pretending to be hitch hiking near the road to lighten our spirits. With a new tire in place, we continued our adventure, shooting (the following) pictures along the way.

The pictures shown below were not enhanced. The cheetah actually jumped onto the lead car of our two safari cars. Recall that the cars have open roofs, which means the people seated in the cars were within just a few feet of the cheetah.

Mary Clare, riding in the rear car, was one of the first to observe the cheetah jumping onto the car ahead of hers. Seeing the big cat, she screamed, "Oh my God, he is going to eat Maura and Megan!"

Jack W. O'Leary & Mary Clare Lyons with Virginia Elizabeth Rose

Maura and John get a close-up view of the big cat.

I began chanting, "Stand up, John, stand up!" to a tune I remembered from the musical *1776*. Soon John was sticking his head out of the open roof and pulling Maura up beside him so she could get a look at the big cat. All the while Megan, I was told, was trying desperately to get under the rear seat of the car. Maura, looking as if she had a clothes hanger holding her mouth wide open, stood with tears streaming down her face. Undaunted, John swung his camera into position and started snapping close-ups of the cheetah.

Eventually it was time to leave the compound and Kenya behind and return home. The nine of us — Sister Mary Brenda, Sarah, Megan, Maura, Mary Clare, John, Jim Ryan, Sr., Jim Ryan, Jr., and I — shared an adventure we will surely remember with great fondness for a very long time.

Leaving Masai Mara.

It's Time To Build St. John The Baptist Church

If one advances confidently in the direction of his dreams and endeavors to live the life which he has imagined, he will meet with a success unexpected in common hours... Build castles in the air, your work may not be lost, that is where they should be. Now put foundations under them.

H.D. Thoreau

During our stay at the hotel in Eldoret, we met with the architect who built the home for disabled children and who had already drawn up plans for the church we hoped to build next to the home. One thing was certain, the church had to be large enough to accommodate up to two-thousand people at one time.

We decided to build the church in honor of Dr. Katherine Keough, former president of St. John Fisher College. Dr. Keough was president of the College for just a few years before she was diagnosed with and then died of cancer. As president, she had continued the program of bringing Kenyan priests to St. John Fisher College. During her term, she took a trip to Kenya where we had a luncheon to meet many of the Fisher graduates.

Upon our return, I approached Dr. Don Bain, the current president of St. John Fisher College, with the idea of dedicating a church in Kenya to Katherine Keough. He agreed to the idea and the College made a significant donation, getting the project off to a good start. Other contributors included the Basilian Fathers, Katherine Keough's son Stephen, Jim Ryan, Sr., Jim Ryan, Jr., John Anderson, Frank Stotz and myself.

When we had what I believed were enough funds to complete the church, I authorized construction to begin. The church, to be named St. John The Baptist, was about halfway completed when we were forced to stop work because of yet another time of uncertainty for Kenya and a frightening outbreak of civil unrest.

The unrest centered in the city of Eldoret near Soy. Following the disputed 2007 election in Kenya, the opposing political parties had started another round of tribal warfare as a way of drawing attention away from the corrupted election.

Apparently, local politicians had distributed drugs and Molotov cocktails to teenage boys, urging them to burn the homes of members of opposing tribes. The area where the church was being built was particularly hard hit by violence, and many homes and buildings were destroyed by the ensuing fires.

Unfortunately, the contractor who was building our church also lost all his building equipment in one of the thousands of fires that turned homes, businesses, churches, medical facilities and other targets into nothing more than ashes.

The turmoil drove about one-thousand people to the parish grounds for safety. We stopped construction of the church and used the money we had raised to care for the refugees now living at the construction site. Most of the refugees were living in the out-of-doors, so we purchased tents for shelter, and the food and medical supplies they couldn't live without.

The old church became a safe haven for women and children during the months of civil unrest. The women and children settle in for one of the night-time sleeping shifts.

Dr. Sue Crawford, entirely on her own, collected and shipped enough hygiene products and medical supplies to fill a forty-foot shipping container for the refugees living at St. John the Baptist Church.

Besides running a medical practice, Dr. Crawford volunteers many hours a week at I.M.E.C. and several weeks a year in third-world countries, volunteering her services along with her doctor husband and their children. I feel humbled when I consider her immeasurable generosity.

Eventually the civil disturbance settled down and the government established camps to take in some of the people displaced during the unrest, while other families returned to their homes to begin the difficult job of rebuilding their lives. Father Protus purchased seeds and fertilizer for the returning farmers so they could replant their fields.

Construction on the church resumed. Obtaining steel girders for the roof took the longest amount of time, but eventually the roof and interior were completed, and the opening ceremony was celebrated July 15, 2011. Among the more than two-thousand attendees were a cardinal, six bishops, several dozen priests, around one-hundred nuns, and even a representative from the Vatican.

St. John The Baptist Church is dedicated in July 2011.

Muthagia Country Club

Sarah Brewin accompanied me to Nairobi during one of my visits to Kenya. She had somehow arranged for us to stay at Muthagia Country Club, a prestigious English men's golf club, which opened its doors on New Year's Eve 1913.

Sarah and I left Nairobi for a few days to check on projects in other areas of the country. Because we would be returning to Nairobi following our visits, I checked a large suitcase that I did not want to take with me on the trip. We informed the bellhop we would return in a few days to pick up the suitcase and left on our trip. When I returned, I gave a clerk at the desk the claim check and asked for the return of my luggage. He asked me to come with him and headed out the door with me following close behind. He took the footpath leading to a large shed-like building behind the club, walked up to the padlocked door, inserted the key into the lock and opened the door. Stepping inside the building, I couldn't conceal my surprise. Lining the entire building in neatly ordered rows were shelves stacked from floor to ceiling with suitcases, steamer trunks, boxes, and every size and type of luggage imaginable.

As the clerk headed to another area of the storage building to look for my bag, I strolled down one of the nearby aisles, reading the luggage tags on the bags stored there as I went along. I was shocked to find tags dating as far back as 1914. There were bags with tags marked with the name, rank and regiment of the English officers who had at one time checked their bags at the club, fully intending to return one day to claim them.

I saw bags that had been tagged and left behind during both World Wars and realized their owners would never return for them as they, themselves, were long gone from this world.

I did not get very far down the aisle before the clerk returned with my bag, firmly telling me to leave the building immediately. I am sure he was uncomfortable with my snooping through the rows of stored luggage left behind so long ago.

Later that night, I spoke with some of the members of the club, all Englishmen who had lived in Kenya for a long time. I asked one man about the shed filled with luggage. He was a bit taken aback, surprised that I was allowed to enter the shed to retrieve my bag. The abandoned suitcases, he said, would remain in the storage shed forever. He confirmed the bags belonged to club members who had stored their belongings at the club for safekeeping and then never returned to retrieve them.

I have often thought about those bags and the stories that could be told about their owners. Most of the men had left their possessions at the club many decades earlier. But throughout the intervening years, the bags remained neatly and securely stored as a sort of testament to those who traveled there before me. Like a buried time capsule, yet a time capsule never to be opened, the bags hold secrets of their long-forgotten owners and remain cloaked in more than a century of the club's own history.

Muthagia Country Club became famous because of the movie *Out of Africa*. A number of scenes in the movie were shot in the club, including the one where Meryl Streep was invited into the men's bar to have a drink. To this day, she is probably one of the only women ever allowed in that bar. In much the same way the locked shed at the rear of the club securely stores luggage left behind by members who will never return, the members hold, preserve and honor both its history and long-held traditions.

Chapter 5
Archbishop Rafael Ndingi of Kenya

Heroes Achieve the Seemingly Impossible

This book would not be complete without sharing a little bit about the life and work of an amazing man, Archbishop Rafael Ndingi Mwana 'A Nzeki.

Fifty years ago, Father Charles Lavery, then president of St. John Fisher College, envisioned an Africa where democracy prevailed.

Although he never realized it, Father Lavery's vision set off a chain of events whose ripples continue to change the present and the future for millions of people. Through the fulfilling of his vision, Father Lavery lives on in the hearts, minds and spirits of the people of Kenya.

Although Kenya's future remains tenuous because of the country's devastating AIDS epidemic, warfare in neighboring countries and a record-breaking drought, hope for Father Lavery's dream, shared by so many others who worked to help make it come true, remains strong and deep.

One who has carried the torch for freedom and democracy, as well as for a more prosperous future for Kenya, is Archbishop Ndingi, one of the first Kenyan priests to participate in President Lavery's educational experience. Archbishop Ndingi's work has helped to lay a new, firm foundation upon which a promising future is being built for his country and its people.

Archbishop Ndingi became Lavery's unrelenting ally in the struggle for freedom and change in East Africa.

For years, Archbishop Ndingi was the most outspoken opponent of the corruption he saw in Kenya's government. Throughout his lifetime, he fought against corruption, political oppression and violence caused by the social and political unrest that overtook Kenya in the country's post-colonial era.

In 2008, President of Kenya Mwai Kibaki assigned the retired Archbishop to chair the governmental committee responsible for resettling the hundreds of thousands of victims left homeless after the civil unrest, which surrounded the elections of 2008.

In 2013, there will be a new national election. Under the country's new constitution and the birth of a new spirit of nationalism, it is the hope of the Kenyan people that this time there will be a peaceful transition to a new era in Kenyan politics.

Born in 1931, the diminutive soft-spoken Rafael Ndingi Mwana A'nzeki was the youngest of five children of a polygamist father who worked as a blacksmith and a mother who raised a family of three daughters and two sons.

In 1941, at the request of his tribal chief, he was enrolled in a Mission Primary School, and in 1945 he was baptized a Roman Catholic Christian.

During World War II, East Africa was war torn and most families had few means and little food. Ndingi's family was no exception. The family had only enough food for just one meal a day. This one meal, their family meal, was served in the evening.

In spite of many hardships, young Ndingi persisted in school. In 1953, he set up a meeting with his father to inform him of his intention to become a priest. At the meeting, his sister asked, "What is a priest?" Ndingi explained that becoming a priest meant that, "I will not have a family... I will be free and open to serve anybody who needs my services."

In traditional Kenyan society, it is the custom for men to have at least one wife. Kenyans would think there was something wrong with a man who did not marry.

His father counseled him, "If you should fail, you should come home and I will give you a wife." And so young Rafael made up his mind. He would enter the priesthood in spite of his family's reservations.

In 1961, Rafael Ndingi was ordained into the priesthood by Bishop John McCarthy, and he soon became known to many people in Kenya through the radio as the announcer on the *Voice of Kenya's Catholic Hour.*

In 1967, at the invitation of Father Lavery, Bishop McCarthy sent Father Ndingi to St. John Fisher College, where he received a Bachelor of Arts in History and Political Science.

While in Rochester, Father Ndingi became close friends with Bishop Fulton Scheen, who is now a nominee for Sainthood. Before Ndingi completed his studies, he received a message from the Vatican that he was to be ordained a Bishop.

As a symbol of Fulton Scheen's respect and friendship for Ndingi, Bishop Scheen gave to him his own gold pectoral cross. Ndingi wore Fulton Scheen's cross around his neck until about seven or eight years ago when, during a struggle for freedom, he was beaten and robbed, and the treasured cross was stolen.

A Voice Unstilled, a biography of Ndingi, describes the reaction of the crowd after Pope Paul VI slipped the Episcopal ring onto the finger of the newly ordained Bishop Ndingi. "Some fixed their gaze on the pectoral cross that hung on his chest while others admired the new vestments that the newly consecrated Bishop was adorned in."

Shortly after returning home to Kenya, Rafael Ndingi became the Bishop of a new Diocese in the Machakos area, and, in 1971, Bishop Ndingi became the first black African Bishop of Nakuru, wherein he focused on recruiting talented students for the priesthood, several of whom followed in his footsteps, going on to earn degrees at St. John Fisher College.

During this time, the hierarchy of the Catholic Church was predominantly white. Bishop Ndingi made it his priority to recruit capable Africans of color into the priesthood to bridge the color gap.

In 1980, he founded Nakuru's seminary. In the early years, seminarians were primarily white. Today in Kenya, the church is primarily black and growing rapidly throughout the country.

Jomo Kenyatta, the first president of Kenya following British rule, was generally supportive of Bishop Ndingi's programs and reforms; however, the winds of change quickly rose when Kenyatta died and Vice President Daniel Moi became president.

Under the rule of President Moi, gross corruption and injustice prevailed. It was Bishop Ndingi who came to be the government's most outspoken, unrelenting, and respected opponent.

In the early 1990s, Bishop Ndingi participated in demonstrations for political reform, emerging as a national leader and becoming the voice of reason and change.

Mysterious circumstances surrounded the deaths of many of Moi's other opponents, and yet the Bishop unabashedly persisted in his criticism of the government. In spite of tragic fates suffered by others, Bishop Ndingi remained faithful to the struggle for political reform.

During the 1997 election, Bishop Ndingi was approached about running for president against President Daniel Moi, but he refused the honor in favor of maintaining his commitment to and his leadership position within the Church. Throughout this time, the Bishop continued to condemn the tribal warfare and raids on non-Kalenjin-tribes (which were principally the Kikuyu people).

During this time of civil unrest, Kikuyu houses were torched, men, women and children were murdered and women were raped. These tragedies were encouraged and supported by the government during a corrupted electoral process.

Bishop Ndingi openly voiced his concern for individuals who were victimized for political, social and/or economic gain, and blamed the government for not intervening on behalf of the people of Kenya. He went as far as to demand the resignation of the government officials and citing their practices as being not only unconstitutional, but immoral as well.

His leadership skills were rewarded under Pope John Paul II. In 1997, Rafael Ndingi became Archbishop of Nairobi.

Archbishop Ndingi demanded constitutional reforms that were eventually ratified in 2010 under the current President Mwai Kibaki. By and large, Archbishop Ndingi is recognized as the leader of the Roman Catholic Church in Kenya at a time when the government of Daniel Moi was doing all within its power to crush the spirit of the people and strip them of their basic human rights.

Sitting in a meeting recently, a Kenyan friend of ours, Father Tuka of Syracuse, New York, said, "Kenyans used to believe that they had no rights, only meager privileges. When the old government used a small portion of funds to build a school, the people thought they were lucky to have access to education. When they had a little money for food, they considered themselves fortunate when the government gave them minimal sustenance. They did not understand that they had any human rights, only privileges."

In referring to Rafael Ndingi, Reverend John Njenga, emeritus Archbishop of Mombasa, said, "In the course of life, you often meet people who distinguish themselves in a way that makes you admire them forever. It may be because of their character, achievement, determination or something so monumental they have done in their lives that their memory lives on forever in the minds of those who meet them."

Because Archbishop Ndingi was so trusted and trustworthy throughout his career, his word went virtually unquestioned. But he was not perfect, he said. He admitted to telling one lie. The lie he told saved the life of human rights activist Dr. Wangari Maathai. He smuggled her to safety at the height of the government's crackdown on human rights. The year was 1993 and the government wished to silence Dr. Wangari. Bishop Ndingi used his car to smuggle her through security checkpoints to safety.

Wangari Maathai, a Kenyan environmentalist who launched The Greenbelt Movement, began her work to reforest her country by paying poor women a few shillings to plant trees. Protecting Kenya's environment, developing a source of firewood, and providing jobs for women, she was also dedicated to creating a democratic Kenya.

Dr. Maathai was described as a feminist, politician, professor, rabble-rouser and human rights advocate. She became the first African woman to win a Nobel Peace Prize. In presenting her with the Peace Prize, the Nobel committee hailed her for taking "a holistic approach to sustainable development that embraces democracy, human rights and women's rights in particular and for serving as inspiration for many in the fight for democratic rights."

Wangari Maathai died in September 2011 at the age of 71, following a lifetime facing down corrupt politicians, being jailed for her activism in support of a democratic Kenya, and having been beaten and left unconscious in the streets while protesting against the Kenyan government's plan to build a skyscraper in Nairobi's only park. Her legacy of hope, however, lives on in Kenya and throughout Africa, where many of her principles are being put into practice today.

In accepting her Nobel Peace Prize, Dr. Maathai said, "In the course of history, there comes a time when humanity is called to shift to a new level of consciousness, to reach a higher moral ground. A time when we have to shed our fear and give hope to each other. That time is now."

Kenya at last appears to be on its way to becoming a full-fledged democracy. Today, a more honest government is leading its nation guided by the new constitution patterned after the Constitution of the United States. Already the people of Kenya are seeing the change in their country. Corruption is down, the judicial system is working, roads are being built, and the entire spirit of the country is uplifted.

Stories From Bishop Ndingi's Den
The Little Church

Bishop McCarthy built a home in Nairobi, Kenya. Later it became home to Archbishop Ndingi. I encountered some of the most accomplished and fascinating people I have ever met in what I have come to think of as "Ndingi's Den."

People from countries near and far came to visit the Archbishop in his home — ambassadors, businessmen, politicians, church leaders, adventurers, and others. Gathering at the house, they came to discuss world affairs. I could write a thousand-page book about the interesting people I met there... If only I could remember them all.

One of these stories includes what Mary Clare and I always called The Little Church. During our visits to Kenya we would pass The Little Church, which is located near Mount Longonot, as we traveled the road from Nairobi to Nakuru. Always fascinated by the quaint little stone church with the red roof, we learned it had been built by Italian prisoners of war sometime between 1942 and 1944.

I first heard the history of The Little Church in Archbishop Ndingi's den.

Italian prisoners of war had built the road that parallels the Great Rift Valley escarpment. The work was nothing short of treacherous slave labor. Learning of the appalling treatment the Italian prisoners of war were forced to endure, Bishop McCarthy became incensed. He made an appointment to speak with the governor of Kenya, which was at that time a colony of the British Empire.

Bishop McCarthy, a unique character, did not ask for accommodations from anyone, instead, he simply told people what they were to do. He was a tough man with a square jaw and imposing manner. He told Governor Sir Henry Moore that the Italians were his friends and proceeded to tell Sir Henry how to treat the Italian captives from that day forward. He also told the governor that he was to ensure the prisoners would be allowed to build a place of worship. And it was so.

The prisoners decided to build a Catholic chapel and the beautiful Little Church was built.

Today people of all faiths visit the church to honor the Italian POWs who died in East Africa during the war. This is also one of the reasons the Italians decided to build Neema Hospital. It was built, in part, to honor the Italian POWs who fought in World War II.

The Check

Another story that flowed out of the Archbishop's den was about a conversation that took place between two bishops.

At one point, Bishop McCarthy visited Bishop Fulton Sheen in New York where he was in charge of a worldwide Catholic charity, the Society for the Propagation of the Faith. Bishop McCarthy needed money for a project and Bishop Sheen was the man to ask. Bishop McCarthy did just that.

Without hesitation, Bishop Sheen wrote a check for $1,000 and handed it to Bishop McCarthy. The check was handed right back to Bishop Sheen with this "request." "Instead of the number one, put the number five in its place and add a zero at the end. I need $50,000." The request was granted.

An HIV/AIDS Pioneer

I remember sitting in the Archbishop's den during one of my visits and hearing about his friend Angelo D'Agostino. The following morning we went to the outskirts of Nairobi to a place called Nyumbani to meet with Angelo.

In 1992, former United States Airforce surgeon and Rhode Island native Reverend Angelo D'Agostino, MD, SJ opened the Nyumbani Home for Abandoned Children with HIV/AIDS on the outskirts of Nairobi. Today, Nyumbani serves more than one-hundred children. Angelo was a surgeon, urologist, psychologist and Jesuit priest all rolled into one.

Angelo said he decided to acquire a medical degree and specialize in urology after he earned his degree in psychology because, "The Jesuits didn't have a need for a psychologist."

A man of great dignity, Father D'Agostino always wore a smile, and in his later years, the short, stocky gentlemen's round face and white beard gave him the appearance of kindly old St. Nick.

Nyumbani Home for Abandoned Children with HIV/AIDS was the first HIV children's home in Kenya. The home consisted of two large red-roofed cottages divided into duplexes, each one bearing the name of a saint. Each duplex included two bedrooms furnished with bunk beds, a sitting room and a kitchen.

The Nyumbani home is a part of a larger compound and community. At the center of the complex is a bright and colorful outdoor play area for the children. The play area is in front of a small building used for group activities and celebrating mass.

The most haunting part of the visit for me was seeing the small graveyard in the corner of the compound. Each grave is neatly marked with a painted white cross, and each simple cross bears the name of a child. All the children buried in the little cemetery had their lives taken from them by AIDS.

Realizing that a home for children would not be sufficient for serving the growing community of adults and children with HIV, Father D'Agostino launched the Lea Toto outreach program in 1998, which provides services to HIV-positive children in the Nairobi area.

The Swahili term Leo Toto means "Raise the child." The outreach program serves approximately three-thousand HIV- positive children and an estimated fifteen-thousand family members with home-based care, counseling, and medical and other services, including nutritional support and training for caretakers.

The outreach program, the brainchild of Father D'Agostino, was a result of a visit he made to Israel where he observed the Kibbutz system. Father D'Agostino envisioned grandmothers caring for up to eleven children in a single household in an attempt to fill the gap created by the loss of almost an entire generation of parents. Some of the children would be the grandmother's own grandchildren and others would be children who had lost their own parents to AIDS.

Bishop Ndingi and I traveled to a community east of Nairobi, spending a day with Father D'Agostino at Nyumbani. I was one of countless visitors and volunteers from the United States, England, Ireland, Italy, Spain and Brazil to experience Nyumbani. Like me, many people visit and become involved in the challenges presented in villages and communities in Kenya. One person at a time, we are all working to help make a difference.

The reason I tell this story now is to share information about Angelo and some of the many things he has done. In my mind, one of his many important life accomplishments was his sharing of information about the AIDS epidemic with Oxford University in England in a time when little was known about HIV and talk of AIDS was taboo.

Much of the data and information uncovered through his work helped to secure support and medicine for those living in his community as well as others. His openness and research have provided invaluable data to the academic community, which continues to help with AIDS prevention and the development of treatment strategies.

Angelo D'Agostino is perhaps most noted for his relentless determination in securing rights and services for the children of Nyumbani. When the government refused to allow children with AIDS to attend school, he sued the government for discrimination. When the cost of medication was too expensive for his families and children to afford, he fought to drive down the costs of antiviral drugs, and in the face of ignorance and fear, he struggled to increase HIV awareness.

Perhaps one of his greatest accomplishments was his unrelenting ability to build a self-sustaining community against insurmountable odds. I also remember him for his kind nature, which endeared him to all who knew him.

Archbishop Ndingi, a good friend of Father D'Agostino, was one of his staunchest supporters. The Archbishop supported Father D'Agostino's positions in the defense of their common goal of caring for the sick and serving the greater community.

Unfortunately, I was never able to revisit Father D'Agostino. Sadly, in 2006, he had a heart attack and passed away.

His good friend Archbishop Ndingi conducted his requiem mass.

To learn more about Father D'Agostino or to become involved in the project or volunteer, visit www. Nyumbani.org.

Jack and Bishop Rafael Ndingi

Part II

Back Home Again

In a society where the rights and potential of women are constrained, no man can be truly free. He may have power but he will not have freedom.
Mary Robinson

Many years after first becoming involved with projects in Africa, Mary Clare and I heard Mary Robinson, former president of Ireland, speak about her experiences in Africa to a capacity crowd that packed the gymnasium at St. John Fisher College.

Mary Robinson worked under Kofi Annan at the United Nations as United Nations high commissioner of human rights. Her experiences in her leadership roles and as an advocate for human rights were fascinating. She shared great insight about her concerns for Africa and its people. Ending her talk, she said, "Africa, she works." Her statement resonates within us to this day.

Africa, she does work. The Kenyan women, whom we have come to know and trust, work hard to protect their children, families and communities. They work in the fields, orphanages, hospitals, schools, clinics and churches to build their own lives and the lives of those they serve with hope and happiness.

In the absence of an effective government, Kenyan clergy and medical workers have provided leadership and guidance to empower people and heal wounds created by decades of tribalism, colonialism, war and civil unrest.

For many organizations, tribalism became the great divide; political and social units are pitted against one another for political, social, and/or economic gain. These rivalries are ingrained and handed down from generation to generation. But what we have noticed is that when two children from different areas, tribes, religions, or backgrounds come together, they do not seem to care about which tribe they are with, where they come from, or what social organization they belong to; they just want to be safe, fed, loved, and, of course, they want to play together.

Kenya is filled with beautiful, capable and wonderful men and women who are doing the right thing — caring for themselves and others — everyday. They do thankless jobs with open hearts and always with smiles on their faces.

Human rights have been expanded in Kenya through the nation's new constitution. Access to education also has been greatly expanded. Those who would otherwise have been relegated to menial labor and low-paying jobs as a means of eking out a living for themselves and their children can now enjoy opportunities to help build a vital Kenya — all because of greater access to education and the lessening of many of the discriminatory practices of the past. For instance, Egerton University was once primarily an institution where only the male children of the wealthy white were allowed to study. Today the ratio of males to females attending Egerton University is about forty-nine percent female to fifty-one percent male. Now that is progress!

Chapter 6

Mary Clare Returns to Kenya

A Different Time, A Different Place

A little more than a decade after our first project collecting and sending textbooks to Kenya, I visited the country accompanied by my older daughter Julia. Although I had previously visited Kenya with Jack, this was Julia's first trip to the land that Jack and I had grown to love. Julia quickly became as enraptured with the natural beauty of the country and the breath-taking views of the mountains, valleys, and awe-inspiring wildlife as we had. But what truly captured her heart was the warmth of the Kenyan people.

A view of the Kenyan countryside along the Great North Road.

The Great North Road runs the length of Africa — all the way from Cape Town at the tip of Africa to Cairo in the north. I talk a lot about roads in this journey because roads are a skeletal structure that supports the body of the continent in much the same way a human skeleton supports a body. During our visits, we drove long distances along this intra-continental highway with Father Stephen as our guide and driver. Our goal was to follow as many tributaries and pathways as possible, giving us the opportunity to photograph some of the places and people that Jack had encountered throughout his visits and adventures in Africa.

As he had other commitments, Jack was unable to attend the grand opening of St. John The Baptist Church and visit with the children of Likiyani Home for Physically Challenged Children. We also planned to visit with the staff of various schools, clinics and hospitals Jack had built or supplied with medical equipment.

Julia and I rose early in the morning for our journey. We would be making stops along the way from Nakuru, where we were staying, to Eldorett. Our primary goal was to visit with the handicapped children in a home near the newly built St. John the Baptist Church in Likiyani. One of the primary reasons for our visit to Kenya was to attend the dedication of the new church. Our first planned stop of the day was a visit at Father Stephen's boyhood home in Mlima.

Since I had never before been to Mlima, I was eager to see how the village fared during the country's most recent civil unrest, which took place in 2007. The uprising destroyed homes, businesses, schools, churches and any other structures that stood in the way of a corrupt political regime desperate to maintain its hold on the country.

After traveling for several miles, we pulled off the main highway onto a clay road riddled with gullies and pot holes, which had in general been worn away from years of use. Deep crevices, created by decades of vehicles driving the well-used road, guided us over rolling hills on the snakelike path that wound through farms and across open fields. Passing travelers, on bikes and on foot, Stephen waved and smiled at each one.

Sometimes he would stop and say hello to the occasional elderly man passing by, leaning heavily on a walking stick. Other times he politely honked and waved at men pulling donkeys laden with sacks of supplies, making their way to hilltop homes.

A few bikes shared the path leading to Stephen's home. These bikes were not the commercial bikes burdened with sacks of rice, maize, chickens and seed that had become a familiar sight as we traveled down the smoother, straight highways. These two-wheeled vehicles carried lone, unencumbered riders up hilly paths toward home.

We stopped and purchased radishes to have with our dinner from this roadside vendor.

Fences and dirt paths divided the land into small farms, creating a patchwork quilt pieced together in squares of deep green, muted brown and vibrant orange.

The larger homes of politicians and members of the Kalenjin tribes seemed out of place in this land of poverty and subsistence, standing tall among the charred remains of the smaller homes of the Kikuru, Kisii and Kamba people.

Many of the smaller homes, torched during the coup, were burned to one degree or another. Some of the homes sustained only minimal damage while others had been burned to the ground. The Red Cross and Danish government had since stepped in and rebuilt the small shacks, replacing traditional wooden roofs with shiny metal ones, giving farmers and their families a home to live in when they returned to reseed their fields and rebuild their lives.

Thousands of tribal people had fled the coup on foot, narrowly escaping their pursuers. Virtually all of their homes had been torched and hundreds of their family members murdered.

According to Stephen, survivors of the coup fled into the bush and up into the hills near neighboring villages, and many others had been relocated to major cities by the government where they began their lives anew.

Stephen estimated that about one-thousand people fell victim to machetes or bows and arrows during the wave of terror in Mlima. Those who returned home in 2008 were deeply traumatized by the deaths of beloved family members and the loss of their homes and livestock.

During a previous visit, I had observed large herds of sheep and cattle, visible from the road, being tended by young shepherds in the far-off fields. Thinking about these herds, I asked Stephen if the villagers' animals are branded. He replied that some animals are branded, but if a mark of ownership appears on an animal, bandits will tear off the animal's flesh to remove the mark of ownership.

"But today is a different time," said Stephen. "With the reconciliation and new constitution, people's wounds are healing and they are slowly returning to their mountain homes."

Stephen then pointed to land off to our right, showing us where his mother's home once stood. Then we looked up to our left where we caught our first glimpse of the newly constructed walls of a church. Father Stephen explained that he was helping to rebuild the village's Presbyterian Church with his friends and neighbors. The church had also fallen victim to the torch. As he finished telling us about the church, the skeletal remains of blackened timber came into view. The timbers are all that remain of the original Presbyterian Church, which had once stood next to St. Paul's Roman Catholic Church.

We pulled into the area in front of St. Paul's and headed for the door to the church. With welcoming smiles, three caretakers greeted us, leading us into the sanctuary where rows of neatly lined pews faced a cement altar still under construction.

No artwork adorned the walls and items that would typically appear on an altar were absent. But the walls, roof, sacristy and, perhaps most importantly, the spirit of the church clearly remained intact. The rest of the church's sacred items had been stolen by bandits.

I marveled that the bandits who stole the sacred objects had allowed the church to remain standing, and that other than the theft of these small items, St. Paul's stood exactly as it had been built years before.

I was pleased the church still stood in spite of the trauma, pain and destruction this small town had endured. Stephen then said something very interesting. He explained that the stone in the walls of the little Catholic Church actually become stronger with age.

I believe the church stands as an enduring symbol and testament to the people of Kenya. Like the very stones in the church walls, they too will only become stronger with time.

We went on our way and at mid-day pulled into an English-style restaurant to enjoy lunch. Stephen called his sister, Mary, to let her know he was on his way to their mother's new house. The family moved Stephen's mother to her new home after his childhood home in Mlima was destroyed during the chaos of the 2007 insurrection.

Having enjoyed a wonderful lunch, we were once again on our way. Driving along the clay paths that lead to Stephen's mother's home, Julia and I reached out of the car windows, grabbing bunches of wild eucalyptus growing along the path. The fragrance filled the car and we breathed deeply the fresh scent.

Stephen explained that he and his six brothers and sisters built their mother's new house after their childhood home in Mlima was torched. The only thing remaining after the fire was the iron gate that for years stood vigil at the front of the house. Since the loss of her home, Stephen's mother had become forgetful and confused. The children, thinking it would help her recognize the new home as her own, moved the gate from Mlima to this new site. The children also replanted their mother's crops and purchased a few small cows to help her feel at home in her new surroundings.

We soon arrived to find Mary waiting to welcome us, swinging open wide the gate that had been so lovingly installed by a devoted family. As I entered the yard, I delighted in the feeling that I, too, had returned home after a long time away.

In front of the house stood Stephen's mother, a beautiful African woman, beaming with a smile that lit up her entire face. Lines creased her face and one of her front teeth was missing, but hers was the most beautiful face I have ever seen. The woman's name is Ester Wambur.

Ester's new home is a wooden rectangle. The dark plaster interior walls are adorned with three large posters, one of which is a picture of Jesus. Sayings such as, "Christ will show you the way" accompany the pictures.

The last time Jack visited Ester, she had scolded her son for not teaching Jack how to speak Swahili while Stephen was living in Rochester. She asked Stephen, "What is it you were doing all that time in America?" Hearing his mom's question, Stephen had let out one of his signature laughs.

It didn't matter that Julia and I didn't understand a single word she was saying, Ester still spoke to everyone in Swahili. Only occasionally would someone translate for her.

Ester sat with Julia throughout our visit, all the while giving motherly advice to her son. One time Stephen translated his mother's words. Looking at Julia, Ester said, "She is so white! She is sick. You leave her here and I will feed her and take her to the doctor."

Julia, whose fair skin was even a bit more pale than usual because of jet lag and fatigue, was completely enamored by Ester, and half of her would have liked to have stayed with her, but being tired and pale were not an excuse to stay and rest in Ester's comfort and care; it was time for us to be on our way. Julia politely asked that her picture be taken with her newly adopted Kenyan grandmother. We took our photographs, then leaving Ester to her work, we headed toward Edgerton University where we would spend the night.

Besides touring Egerton University, we spent a great deal of our time in Kenya visiting several primary and secondary schools. In the center of Nakuru, we toured Christ the King Secondary School, a one-story, quad-style girl's school located not far from the Central Office of the Diocese of Nakuru.

Most secondary schools in Kenya are on a trimester schedule; this school is no exception. In spite of its age and the fact it is greatly overcrowded, Christ the King is, in my view, the most impressively run facility we visited on our tour. From a financial standpoint, the school is fully self sustaining.

There is an overall feeling or vibration you get when you walk through a well-run organization. I recognized this school as one of those well-run organizations the moment I passed through the school's front gates.

Arriving at Christ the King, we were directed through a side gate by the school's guard, then escorted by one of the nuns from the diocese, who was accompanied by an administrative aid, to the principal's office where we met Sister Virginia.

Sister Virginia is principal of Christ the King and an empowered African woman who personally led us through classrooms, dormitories, bathing facilities, and the schools old kitchen and dining areas. She proudly pointed out the new kitchen and cafeteria areas. Sister carefully guided us over and around debris, nodding to the laborers who were working on the newly constructed rooms. We took note of the commercial-quality appliances standing at the ready for their first use.

Because Nakuru is the fastest growing city in Kenya, this popular school is in high demand and overcrowded. As we made our way across the grounds and through the buildings, we noticed that every classroom was occupied by students busily engaged in their school work. In the dormitories, crisply made bunk beds lined the walls, and trunks, holding the students belongings, stood neatly packed at the foot of the bunks. A net was draped over each of the bunks; placed there to protect sleeping students from night-roaming, malaria-bearing mosquitoes.

Malaria, carried and spread by mosquitoes, is still a leading cause of illness and death throughout Africa. Mosquitoes, avoiding the heat of day, feed primarily in the relative cool of the night. A simple mosquito net is a proven lifesaver for both children and adults.

To the rear of the campus, Sister Virginia pointed out her own small house and the school's sports fields that lie beyond. To the right of the fields we saw a number of houses much too small to be homes for people. We were told these small structures housed the school's guard dogs. At night, the guard dogs are sent to patrol the perimeter of the campus, ensuring that no one enters the grounds. No dogs were in sight. Sound asleep in their houses, they would not emerge until evening when they would resume their important duty of patrolling and protecting the campus compound.

To the back of the kitchen we observed a pump connected to a recently dug well where students wash their clothes in the fresh flowing water — a true luxury. Beyond, the abundant gardens appeared ready for harvesting. The school's older students are taught how to plant the fields as a part of a senior project. Looking out across the land, we saw girls in their school uniforms and brightly colored sweaters dotting the surrounding fields, hearing the girls chatting and laughing as they worked.

We entered the school, and to our surprise, we soon realized we were already a part of this wonderful place. In the school's library, Julia spotted red math books lined up side by side on one of the bookshelves. She ran to the shelf and opened up one of the books. It was unmistakable. Proudly, Julia exclaimed, "This is my old math book!" And, indeed it was. We were delighted to see the books we had worked so hard to gather, sort, and pack years before had arrived at their destination and were being used by these eager young women.

A pattern of events began to unfold as we travelled from place to place, school to school. At Egerton University, I spotted the history books I once used for teaching ninth grade global studies. And when driving along the roads, we passed schools whose names were familiar. These schools had sent us thank-you notes for the books we had sent them more than a decade before, telling us how important these same textbooks, cast-offs from Western New York school systems, were to the children of Kenya.

This Place He Calls Home
Stephen's House at Egerton University

In 1939, Lord Maurice Egerton of Tatton established Egerton as an agricultural school for British subjects with a land grant of seven-hundred and forty acres. The Government added to the land surrounding Egerton University, increasing the school's property to four-thousand acres. Across the street from the university's front gates sit roadside merchants, wooden shacks and plaster buildings. Stephen's house is one of the buildings on the Egerton campus.

Seeing Stephen's car nearing the grounds, the Egerton University guard immediately waived him in. Stephen turned off the main road and headed down a secondary road leading to a corrugated tin gate. It is the responsibility of one of the school's graduate students who lives in a small building behind the main facility to open the gate for visitors.

Gardens, neatly organized and beautifully maintained, surround the university buildings. To the left of the house rose gardens in full bloom, and large poinsettia trees filled the front yard. The purple flowers of a vinca vine graced the ground near my feet as I stepped out of the car, and an enormous cactus tree stood vigil in the side yard where arborvitaes defined the lot line. In the center of the drive, were a bottle bush tree and hibiscus bushes. On the lower levels of the yard, a variety of plants, including wandering jews and spider plants, appeared to be thriving in their natural environment.

Stephen's stone and plaster house was built in the 1960s. Typical of the era, the windows are framed with leaded glass.

We drove around to the back of the house where coops for roosters and chickens stood nearby. Chickens that were most likely supposed to be inside the coops, roamed freely about the grounds.

Entering the house, we were greeted by Stephen's housekeeper, a woman everyone calls Mamasan. Mamasan offered us a seat and immediately disappeared into the kitchen where she busily prepared a dinner of maize, rice, peas and chicken. I couldn't help but wonder if the chicken she was preparing for our meal was a relative of the others roaming the grounds outside.

While Julia and Stephen enjoyed refreshments and watched television, I studied the room. On one of the bright red and yellow walls hung a painted portrait of Ester. The inscription beneath the painting proclaimed, "To the world she is one woman; to me she is the world." Stephen said the portrait had been painted by a local artist.

Looking for a novel to read, I turned my attention to the bookshelves lining the walls. As I perused the shelves, I was surprised to find them filled mostly with text books bearing titles such as *Clinical Psychology* and *Cognitive Psychology*. Thinking that was a bit deeper reading than I wanted to pursue just then, I headed to my quarters to unpack and take a brief nap. The next thing I knew, I was waking up to a new day.

The Nakuru-Solai Highway runs for hundreds of miles, wandering through small towns and open spaces across Kenya. We left early one morning, driving the highway on a visit to the outskirts of Solai and Bahati.

We headed first to St. John's Cottage Hospital with additional plans to visit some of Stephen's newest project sites.

Stephen had just completed building a small school, which quickly filled to capacity. In the words of J. Lyons, "They came, so we built."

Children crowd around the front door of Father Stephen's school, trying to catch a glimpse of their visitors.

Father Stephen decided the school was a good place to hold worship services and soon he was celebrating weekly Sunday Mass in the classrooms.

But it wasn't long before Father Stephen decided to build a new place of worship, and so began collecting money to build a church out of stone that would be called St. Gabriel's. Able to raise about $200 every six months, which pays for about two layers of stone, Stephen is building the church with the help of members of his community. The stones forming the walls of the church are neatly organized and beautifully maintained. He has been working on the project for more than seven years and hopes to be able to complete the church within the next two years.

Father Stephen builds a new church two layers of stone at a time.

We continued on our way through small towns, weaving and dodging in and out of traffic, including other vehicles, bicycles, pedestrians and beasts of burden. Julia and I decided it might be a good idea to rename Father Stephen, Father Kamikaze, in honor of his unique driving technique.

At one point, Stephen asked Julia to look to the right as he pointed to a building that had been closed for many years.

He explained to Julia that the building had been a tavern named SMIRNOFF'S after the popular brand of vodka, and that during one of Jack's previous visits Jack had ordered rounds and rounds of vodka for everyone the tavern that night. Shortly thereafter the Kenyan government forced the owner to shut down his establishment. Father Stephen didn't provide any details concerning the incident that provoked the government to take such drastic action, but knowing Jack, his celebration with his Kenyan friends was the tavern owner's undoing. The fun had to have been taken to the max as the details of that evening remain fresh in Father Stephen's mind even to this day.

We moved on and Father Stephen pointed out another building called the White House. This roadside building listed the names of the presidents of the United States on its front façade, and we could see various United States constitutional rights inscribed on the side walls. Stephen explained that the business was a popular tavern, and since the "crazy American" had caused the shut down of SMIRNOFF'S, the White House is now the only tavern remaining in the area. Stephen pondered the thought, "The owner of the White House must have been pleased at the turn of events, thinking, 'Thanks a lot, Jack.'"

He explained the owner of Kenya's White House was once an orphan saved from a life in the streets by an American sponsor. The one-time street orphan, so delighted by the help he received in his childhood, openly and very publicly celebrates his love for America by displaying a list of the names of every American president on the front of his building.

Kenya's White House bar has the name of every American President written on the front of the building, a tribute to the generosity of the American sponsor who save the bar's owner from a life of poverty and despair.

Further along on our journey Stephen pointed out a farm belonging to Kenya President Kibaki. President Kibaki appears to be a good leader, intent on building a strong and honest government. There is much evidence that leads us to believe Kenya is building an infrastructure that will support the country's development. Clearly President Kibaki is paving the way to a better future one road at a time.

Just four years ago, Kenya's infrastructure was in a state of near collapse. Today, trucks loaded with goods travel Kenya's superhighways from the ports of Mombasa to the roads of Central Africa day in and day out.

From our roadside vantage point, President Kibaki's sprawling farm appeared in need of a bit of work itself. Passing by the farm, Stephen considered the condition of the property, offering the recommendation that the president not plan to take up farming in his retirement. With tongue in cheek, I wished Mr. Kibaki well and hoped for him a nice retirement package from his day job as president of Kenya.

St. John's Hospital Ten Years Later

Today, St. John's Cottage Hospital provides medical care to almost one-thousand people every month. The electric lines that we ran into the area when we built the hospital provide electricity not just to the hospital, but to the local residents in this Bahati hamlet as well. Over all, the people are healthier and wealthier because of the infrastructure improvements the clinic project brought to the area.

Touring the facility, we learned the electricity also provides refrigeration, enabling the clinic's administrators to provide vaccines and medicines that require refrigeration. These serums are routinely administered to prevent and treat common ailments that, left untreated, could prove to be life threatening.

Fredrick Kariuki, one of the hospital's administrators, toured the complex with us, telling us people arrive at the clinic with illnesses that include tuberculosis, malaria and pneumonia. He mentioned that earlier in the week the clinic staff delivered several babies and that the need for preventative care in the hamlet remains critical.

While we were touring the hospital, a young man rode up on a motor bike. I learned he was an ambulance driver. By ambulance driver, I mean he transports patients to the care facility on the back of his motor bike. Somehow he had fallen from his motor bike and his leg, which had been torn and scraped, had became septic. Before leaving the hospital, in keeping with his character, Father Stephen reached into his pocket and paid for the young man's treatment.

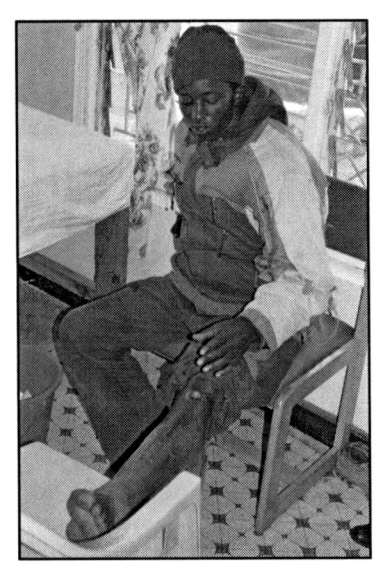

A patient receives treatment at St. John's Cottage Hospital, and curious children run to the hospital's gate to check us out as we tour the area.

The Tea Farm Today

Kenyan tea is considered to be one of the world's finest. We learned that since our last visit to Kenya, tea workers wages have increased from what was the equivalent of one dollar a day to about three dollars a day – a tremendous boost to the tea workers and their families.

Julia and I both wanted to take photos of the laborers working the fields. But over the years, the tea farmers have become uncomfortable being photographed by strangers. Sadly, they were taught the difficult lesson that not everyone can be trusted. They have become fearful of being photographed and exploited by their government and by other, non-government agency personnel. Heeding Father Stephen's warnings to keep any photography low key, we honored the tea workers' privacy and remained in our car, taking just a few pictures from a respectful distance.

Neema Hospital Today

Today a Neema Hospital patient pays $2 per visit. Even at this low cost the facility is not only profitable, it is growing.

The European Union has invested extensively in the hospital since our last visit. When Julia and I visited the new hospital's maternity building where prenatal and postnatal care is provided, we saw incubators for the care of newborns had recently arrived. New equipment from places like the Netherlands and Germany had recently been installed throughout the facility. As we toured the new operating suite, I realized it was as well equipped as any I have ever seen. I thought to myself, "This is a miracle." Gabriele is doing a fabulous job as CFO and numerous plans for future expansion are already well under way. Gabriele mentioned that the hospital was also in need of an ambulance for transporting patients.

Making Our Way to Nakuru

If this priest thing does not work out, you might try being a driver.
Mary Clare Lyons

Nairobi, the capitol of Kenya, is home to about four-million people and is about one-hundred-forty kilometers from Nakuru, one of the fastest growing cities in Africa. The road from Nairobi to Nakuru was once a snakelike road full of potholes and dangerous turns, but not anymore.

Stephen picked us up at 10 o'clock one morning for a drive to Nakuru. He wanted to stop along the way for a visit with his mother. Stephen explained, "It used to take four hours to travel this path, but today it takes just over one-and-one-half hours to make the same journey."

Chinese corporations are rebuilding roads and infrastructure in Kenya at an incredible rate. Following the bloody insurrection that ravaged Kenya in 2007, rebuilding the nation has become a priority.

The former minister of transportation had destroyed some of the nation's major roads under the Moi regime because he owned a small fleet of airplanes and was busy building his own fortunes. His transportation business, a virtual monopoly, was a highly profitable operation where wealthy tourists and businessmen would choose to fly his airline when visiting game reserves and distant cities, instead of making arduous trips by motor vehicle.

Stephen acknowledged that the new government has made great gains over the years from a corruption and infrastructure standpoint. Acknowledging these changes in his country, he said, "The people now wonder what the government did before."

The main road from Nairobi to Nakuru hugs the Great Rift Valley Escarpment with some of the most beautiful scenery and farmland in the world. We passed through valleys dotted with small towns and open plains. As we left the more populated areas, Mount Longonot came into view, and we stopped to peer down into the seemingly endless valley below where the land divided, then fell to great depths, and stretched on for hundreds of miles into the distance.

Stephen wove through town after town, each uniquely adorned with brightly colored buildings. We stopped for fuel at a gas station in one of the towns. Both Julia and I spotted a small child standing barefoot on a smoldering pile of trash. The child poked at the trash with a stick in much the same way my own children used to when they were small and had found something of interest on the ground.

I thought back to when my children were young — maybe two or three years old — and we would take walks, starting with the sidewalk in front of our house. Before we could take more than a few steps one of the girls would stop to inspect a worm, a wad of gum, or a wrapper, wanting to poke at it or pick it up. I would hurry them along the path and scold them, saying, "Do not touch that." Or "Don't put that dirty thing in your mouth." This child stood alone with no adult nearby. Absorbed in his activity, he poked about until he finally lost interest and eventually wandered over to the path beside the road.

Leaving the town behind, we passed through the flat plains of Lord Delamere's estate. Lord Delamere, born in 1870, was a British-born pioneer farmer, socialite and hunter. He lived, loved, and partied in the heyday of the Kenyan highlands. When he died in 1931, his children and grandchildren took over the ownership and management of the sprawling estate.

The main road slices through the Delamere Ranch, which spans more than fifty miles in length and spreads out about fifty miles on either side of the road. Some of the Delamere family members are a group of "nutters," according to what I have read. Nutters are not nut farmers, as one might think. Nutters is an English term used to describe people who appear a bit out of control. One article I read about the family highlighted one of the grandsons and his recent run-ins with the law. The grandson, convicted of shooting and killing a game warden and sent to jail, had recently been released from his incarceration. According to the local newspapers, the widow of the game warden was outraged by the grandson's early release.

Shortly after we passed Mount Longonot, a beautiful church came into view. I remembered what Jack had said about The Little Church and how Italian prisoners of war had not only constructed much of this road, but had built the church as well. The prisoners had literally carved the church out of the surrounding rock.

We moved along the road, turning our attention to our stretch of the highway where, during the dry season, monkeys seeking food and water move in closer and closer, hoping food will be tossed to them from passing vehicles. It's routine for tourists and other passersby to feed the monkeys or leave behind food for them to find. The monkeys have learned to lay in wait for passing cars and the delights that are sure to come their way from the generous passengers riding inside. But it is now July and the rainy season is upon us as we travel through the area and the monkeys are nowhere in sight.

Years After My First Visit, It's a Different World

When I returned to Nakuru, I was surprised to see people were no longer digging ditches and laying pipe by hand. Instead, large equipment shipped in from China is changing the face of the nation. Today the Chinese are building highways — including overpasses and underpasses to handle the traffic; something not needed just a few short years ago. The changes that have taken place in the years since we last visited Kenya are startling to me. The building of the nation's infrastructure is beyond belief. One outcome of all this building is that the new roads are making for fairly easy access to the nation's rich mineral resources.

The people of Kenya are seeing how the new roads are changing their country's landscape and are happy with their new government. These changes are creating an atmosphere of optimism for the future.

A Visit With The Little Sisters of St. Francis

The Little Sisters of St. Francis live in a gated compound in a small town called Bahati. Bahati's climate is warmer than the higher elevations where tea is grown. However, like other communities in Kenya, the backbone of the economy in Bahati is agriculture.

Stephen, Julia and I made a trip to visit The Little Sisters, arriving at our destination late in the day. We wanted to spend some time with the sisters at the Bahati novitiate and to meet Sister Theresa, the current Mother Superior.

Drawing closer to the novitiate, we passed young girls who appeared to be high-school age. They were walking along the road and heading to the buildings where the nuns live and study. We pulled up in front of the main building and climbed the steps to the front door where we waited for one of the sisters to welcome us in. Young girls in school uniforms and sweaters scurried along the paths crisscrossing the property, stealing curious looks at us from behind the books they carried.

It was only moments before the door opened and a young woman invited us in. She led us down a hallway, through an open courtyard, and into a sitting room beyond. Soon Sister Theresa, face radiant, entered the room and welcomed us with genuine pleasure.

Sister, a warm and gracious woman with a beautiful smile and skin the color of rich milk chocolate, moved with grace and ease. We were immediately comfortable in her presence. She engaged us in conversation and charmed us with her delightful sense of humor.

We learned from Sister Theresa that The Little Sisters order was founded by a nun known as Sister Kevin and that there were currently twenty-two novices preparing to become nuns and join the order. Becoming a nun requires about four years of study, much like earning a college degree.

The Little Sisters of St. Francis is a teaching order and many of the women entering the order go on to pursue careers as teachers, social workers and counselors.

Already long-time friends, Stephen and Sister reminisced. Recounting their shared stories with Julia and me, they sprinkled jokes into the conversation along the way.

When our introduction to the life of a nun living in Kenya was complete, Sister invited us into the kitchen for tea.

Only a few religious pictures and other items adorned the otherwise pale, barren walls of the dining area. Filling the room's center was a long wooden table surrounded by many wooden chairs. A plate of fresh round bread and containers of tea had already been placed at either end of the table.

Sister directed us to our places at one end of the table and soon nuns were entering the kitchen and filling up the empty chairs.

What followed was a lively discussion punctuated by much laughter as we sipped our tea and sampled the delicious breads.

Sister invited us to see the order's chicken coop, cattle sheds and growing fields that stretched out behind the facility. These are projects we funded during a previous visit to Kenya, which are vital to providing food for the novitiate.

In the area around the chicken coop, the sisters keep not only chickens, but rabbits and ducks as well. Soon the sisters were teaching Julia and me how to handle untamed rabbits. Unsuccessful at mastering this task, I giggled as a small rabbit escaped my hold and attempted to climb into my shirt.

The proper technique for handling wild rabbits is to lift the critter by its ears, but I was happy to simply hold my little rabbit in the palm of my hand. Stephen and Julia were more successful at holding their rabbits. Stephen reached down and picked up a small rabbit by its ears. All the while the little fellow's feet kicked madly about. Julia mastered the skill of keeping her little critter under control after just a few tries.

A city girl who had not spent much time in the agricultural communities of the world, Julia marveled at the cows, pigs and neatly planted gardens. She walked through the compound snapping pictures of the farm animals and abundant crops growing in the fields.

I noticed the lens of Julia's camera focused on a young woman working in the field. The young woman, one of the novitiates, worked steadily, deftly turning the soil with a hoe she held in her hands.

Rain suddenly began to fall, shortening our tour of the grounds. We hurried for shelter and then to our car parked in front of the compound. The Sisters invited Julia to come back and spend more time at the novitiate and she was excited at the prospect of returning sometime in the near future. The Sisters promised that when she returned they would teach Julia how to milk a cow. We said our farewells and headed back down the hill to the Great North Road.

A novice at work in the fields. Today, there are twenty-two young women studying to become nuns in the order of The Little Sisters of St. Francis.

Mary Clare and Julia Continue Their Journey

Next stop on our journey was St. John The Baptist Church. As we headed toward Eldoret, my attention was drawn to the burned-out ruins of buildings, standing like blackened skeletons beside the road. Soon I was counting the number of new tin roofs on small houses that had sprung up since the country's violent unrest had subsided. Feeling sleepy, I began to yawn, thinking that perhaps counting tin roofs was somewhat like counting sheep. Father Stephen saw me yawn and said the altitude seemed to be getting to me. Eldoret is high above sea level where the air is thinner, and I was yawning to increase the oxygen flow to my lungs. He explained it is quite common for people to repeatedly yawn at these altitudes and that many cross-country runners come to this part of the world to train for their competitions. This is why Kenyan runners are among the best in the world. Pretty much their entire training is done at these high-altitudes.

Some of the towns we passed through appeared to be especially hard hit by the rampage that ravaged the area, and yet other homes and towns seemed virtually untouched.

Suddenly, a tent community came into view and I asked Stephen to pull over so we could take a closer look. Clearly nervous about doing so, he cautiously agreed.

The first thing I noticed about the tent city was the two stone walls standing erect in the center of the hundreds of tattered tents. Inside the stone walls a battered old man sat on a step that led to an open doorway. It looked like the door itself had been long gone, leaving behind nothing more than an empty gap.

Julia wanted to get out of the car to take a picture of the scene. Stephen urged her to make it quick. As Julia jumped out of the back seat of the car, I turned to see a beautiful black girl holding her children and standing near the side of our car. She was no more than 15 or 16 years old, but already she had two small children to care for. I smiled at her and she cautiously looked at me. She was clearly afraid. It also was evident she had nothing — no food, no home, nothing at all except the clothes on her back. Her children's clothes were in tatters.

My Road to Kenya

Not realizing what I was doing, I reached into my pocket and took out what money I had there. I reached out and handed the money to the young mother, money she needed to help feed her children.

A young woman with her child stands amongst ruins along the road to Eldoret. Nearby is a Red Cross tent city. The young woman is being carefully watched by the man in the background.

At first she looked at me in disbelief and then when she realized that I wanted nothing from her, that I only wished her well, her eyes filled with tears. Then she nodded and smiled. It was her way of saying thank you.

Suddenly others from the tent city who had been watching us from a distance stormed our car, begging for money. Stephen yelled to Julia to get in the car as he handed out a few hundred shillings to some of the crowd now pressing into the sides of the car. Stephen stomped the accelerator and we sped off down the road.

On the way to Eldoret, I noticed a newspaper on the back seat of Stephen's car. Across the masthead was written *National Mirror*. The paper was dated March 2011.

The headlines read, "Where is Justice for IDPs?" In the middle of the page was a picture of a white tent with a small boy wearing a necktie standing nearby. In front of the tent sat a woman who appeared to be the boy's mother. I asked Stephen what the initials IDP stood for. He answered, "Internally Displaced Person." The tent in the picture looked much like the tents we had observed along the road.

I read the article and wondered that if there is justice in Kenya for these people, why do they still live in tattered tents along roadsides? The article quoted a man named Zacchaeus Okoth, a member of a committee called the Justice and Peace Commission. I learned he is also an Archbishop in the Catholic Church. The article quoted him. "... IDPs have been stripped of their constitutional right as provided for in Art. 28 of the Constitution of Kenya: every person has inherent dignity and the right to have that dignity respected and protected. We remind the government that the Church has the responsibility to ensure that every person has the right to quality healthcare, adequate housing, reasonable standards of sanitation, sufficient and quality food, water and social security."

The article claimed that it is the Commission's calling to remind those with political power it is their responsibility to morally represent the people of Kenya and solve social problems. It never occurred to me that politicians might not understand this to be an obligation of their elected office.

The Archbishop later revealed a concern that as politicians are gearing up for the 2013 election, there are fears that media and government will once again stir up ethnic tension as a means of maintaining their power over the nation. He fears the ethnic tensions would lead to civil unrest, and in turn, the civil unrest would make it necessary to call off the elections, which would in turn maintain the status quo.

The Road to Likiyani Children's Home and St. John the Baptist Church

As we drew closer to Eldoret and Likiyani, I noticed fewer and fewer houses with the new tin roofs I had seen earlier in our drive. In the outlying towns there were entire areas where the Red Cross had come in and built new homes with the now familiar shiny new corrugated tin roofs. The new homes were easy to spot as rays from the sun glinted off their tin roofs. The people living in these homes were fortunate; they had survived the violence of the civil unrest and the fires

My Road to Kenya

that blazed across the land. Others still wait for homes for themselves and their families.

I remembered seeing a documentary about Eldoret and the many people who were burned to death in a church during the 2007 insurrection. I thought of the new tin roofs as some sort of evidence that the people of Kenya have not only the will to survive but the indomitable strength to overcome the most difficult of conditions. I understood their joy in simply living their lives today — as simple and basic as they are — and their hope for a better future.

We drove into the city of Eldoret and looked for the Nakumatt Store where we had arranged to meet Father Protus Hamisi. While looking for the store, I noticed many of the buildings lining the street seemed to be empty. Father Stephen explained the buildings were abandoned because the government warned many tribes like the Kikuru that their people should leave the villages and towns just prior to the insurrection. Most of the people had indeed fled to the larger cities like Nakuru to escape the burning and killing they knew was about to take place.

It struck me as odd that Father Protus had so many people in his congregation in Likiyani who took refuge in the countryside, and I asked myself why people would go further into the interior where the trouble had begun rather than leave the area and resettle in Nakuru.

We arrived in Likiyani and were dumbstruck by the size of the new church and the vastness of the campus where the Children's Home had been built. Clearly, the vast majority of people had chosen to stay in the same area where they and their ancestors had made their home generation after generation. The people were connected to the land and committed to their communities, and they would not be easily displaced from their homes.

Our first sight of St. John The Baptist Church happened as we entered the town of Likiyani. The church itself stands like a small cathedral or basilica outlined against Kenya's vivid blue sky.

Father Protus greeted us as we stepped from our car, proclaiming the grand opening of St. John's would take place in a week. But as we toured the unfinished church, we could not imagine how it could possibly be completed within such a short time. It appeared to us that it would take at least a month to complete the finishing touches. The pews had not yet even been delivered and the altar remained unfinished.

Father Protus boasted that Cardinal John Njue was to preside at the celebration mass. He apologized for the construction delays, citing the Archbishop's heart surgeries and the most recent insurrection and its local refugee problem as reasons for reported cost overruns, as well as the delays in meeting building deadlines. He told us his life had been threatened several times during the unrest because he had offered refuge to people from Lugari, Soy, Kitale, Turbo and Eldoret.

We were grateful the church was almost finished and happy the town of Lukiyani was once again in a state of peace. In spite of the grand nature of the St. John The Baptist building project, what stands out for me as the most beautiful part of the house of worship is its tabernacle. The beautiful tabernacle had been proudly unwrapped from its packing materials and reverently placed on the altar.

The tabernacle, made of ceramic and hand-crafted by a local artisan, had been fashioned into a small hut resembling the Kenyan farm huts that line the roads to and from the town. A cross of painted gold topped the hut, and the key hole on the hut's door was adorned with an escutcheon in the shape of a small ear of corn. Corn, known as maize, is the primary food of the people of Kenya. The symbolic brilliance of this little hut took my breath away. As maize nourishes the people's bodies, worship nourishes their souls.

Julia took pictures of the new church while I spoke with Father Protus. We watched as his helpers put into place the statues of Joseph and Mary, framing the pulpit. The beautiful figures were traditional visages, ordered from elsewhere, and I was a little disappointed that the local artist who created the tabernacle was not given the opportunity to create these statues as well. I noticed a large cross with the figure of Jesus on it resting on the floor in the center of the church. I envisioned the cross lifted high and mounted on the wall behind the altar.

Father explained that thousands of people would attend the dedication as now twelve-hundred students, of which fifty were the handicapped children that we support and for whom we built the new home, attended the compound's educational institutions. The students' parents and families, as well as local politicians, had all been invited to join in the celebration.

Our tour took us past the old church still standing nearby, and Father Protus said, "The old church is being converted into a teacher's college. Its pews and fixtures are being sent to an older, less fortunate parish."

We headed down a dirt path to the main road and children began to follow us. Soon the group of curious children had grown quite large, and we began to talk with them as we made our way to the Children's Home. We entered the grounds of the children's home and found the building much the same as we had left it years before. One exception was that the center room inside the building was now filled with teachers conducting a meeting. In the children's living areas, we found the handicapped children eating their lunches of beans and maize. Some of the children were playing while others sat quietly on their beds, but the one thing they all shared was that every one of them was laughing.

Jack W. O'Leary & Mary Clare Lyons with Virginia Elizabeth Rose

Holy Family Orphanage
So Much Need, Yet So Much Joy

Mary Ellen, a friend of mine and a supporter of The Helpers of Mary in Syracuse, New York, asked if I would visit the children's home the organization built in a town called Barut, Kenya. Barut is located on the outlying edge of Nakuru. I told Mary Ellen I would visit the home, and so after visiting St. John The Baptist Church, we headed for Barut.

During our drive from Egerton to Barut, Father Stephen told us that our stay at the orphanage would have to be brief. It was already getting late in the day and when the sun sets in this section of town, he explained, the roads become dangerous.

Behind the walls and shrubs lining the main street to Barut lie dilapidated, make-shift homes that shape the slums where many of the area's poor live. Wherever there is poverty, there also are desperate people. Stephen feared the night bandits who stalk this road would be looking for travelers to rob. Nervous and concerned for our safety, he did not want us to stay long.

Road blocks are common in Kenya. Travelers often come upon metal bars armed with spikes placed across the roads. In years past, corrupt police personnel manned these types of roadblocks, collecting so-called tolls from travelers. Today in Kenya, most of the roadblocks serve as security check points, and it is common to see armed officers stationed at these stops. Inspecting suspect vehicles is part of the government's clamp down on road piracy. Stephen explained to us that the new government is deeply concerned about bandits and piracy, and that the borders of Somalia and Ethiopia are not secure. Pirates and illegal immigrants are crossing the porous borders, setting up shop along Kenya's roadways.

Stephen warned us that if we came upon any roadblocks in this one particular section of road, we most likely were being stopped by pirates. He said if anyone attempted to stop him in this area of the highway, he would hit the gas and not look back. Forewarned of the danger we could encounter on the road in the dark of night, we committed to leaving the orphanage well before nightfall.

The orphanage is in an impoverished area and is located directly across the street from St. Luke's Boy School. St. Luke's was one of the schools to receive a large shipment of books from the donations from Western New York in 2003. I was surprised to learn that St. Luke's sits right across the street from the new orphanage.

We arrived at the orphanage and were directed to pull our car around to the back, where a young man stood at the ready to unlock the gates from the inside.

Holy Family Orphanage is configured by a handful of buildings arranged to create a small court yard. One of the buildings serves as a dormitory for the older children. In front of the building, a small plot of grass fashioned into the shape of a heart was framed by small white stones. To our delight, we were greeted at the doorstep by a string of cut marigolds, arranged to spell out the word "WELCOME."

The children, upon seeing our van, piled out of the dormitory door to greet the arriving strangers. Stephen stepped out of the van first to greet the Sisters in charge of the home. Julia and I greeted the children with handshakes and hellos. Sister Alphonsa, the director of the home, a slight, middle-aged woman of Indian heritage, introduced herself and asked if the children could sing to us.

The children proceeded to sing their songs in both Swahili and English. They sang religious songs in Swahili and they sang songs of happiness in English. Some of the children seemed playful and happy. Others, who attended school all day, were by this time tired and hungry.

I saw a new building off to my left and, nearby, a woman washing children's clothes in buckets of soapy water. Sister Alphonsa asked us to be the first visitors to see the new building and the babies being cared for there. We learned from our friends in Syracuse that the nuns had just started taking in babies, and that most of the babies and children in this home were either abandoned or were left orphaned when their parents died of AIDS.

Passing a woman sitting on a simple wooden chair holding a small child, we entered the building. The bare interior walls had been painted a muted beige. The fluorescent lights suspended from the ceilings provided only minimal light, creating a sense of darkness rather than subdued light. We made our way down the darkened hall to the nursery, where we found five babies lying on their backs in five separate cribs.

The smallest baby was no more than two months old. She was tightly bound in a blanket and wore the small cap of a newborn on her head. The infant's tiny face was red and she held her eyes and mouth firmly shut and kept them that way throughout our entire visit. It seemed like she was sleeping, but the expression on her face appeared to be tightly held as if she were squinting in a perpetual pout. I was afraid to touch and hold the tiny baby, and so left her lying there alone in her crib. After we left the home, I was sorry I hadn't held her when I had the chance.

Vincienne and Vincent, two baby boys, appeared to be about five months old. They slept in a pair of cribs against the wall. In the crib in the center of the room, Peter lay on his back staring at the ceiling. I instinctively held out my hands, taking him into my arms. He remained expressionless and rigid as I held him close to me. I felt like I was holding an inanimate object instead of cuddling an infant. I knew this precious little boy believed deep down inside that he had been rejected and abandoned, and that he was unloved. But nothing could have been further from the truth. I had fallen in love with him the moment I set eyes on this sweet baby boy.

I have held hundreds of children and never before felt a child hold itself so yardstick stiff. The nuns explained that the children needed human interaction for them to develop normally. These children need lots of love to reverse the wrongs that have been done to them.

I placed Peter back in his crib and one of the nuns picked up Peter's twin sister Dorcass and placed her in the same crib with her brother. Dorcass quietly lay on her side of the crib. Her face held the same expressionless gaze as Peter. Sister Alphonsa explained that she sometimes places the two babies in the same crib together so they have one another for company.

My Road to Kenya

As Julia held and rocked a number of the children, it was clear she was falling in love with them too. As I watched her, I noted that she was a natural at giving the babies the love and care they needed, much like a seasoned mother gives her love to all her children.

At one point in our visit, Julia took a long, thoughtful look around the room, telling us that what the room needed was color — lots of color — to help stimulate the children's brains.

Julia and I talked about purchasing mobiles to place over the babies' heads so the children had something to draw their attention and arouse their curiosity. I looked around for a rocking chair, and saw none. I asked Sister if the children had baby swings and she said they had nothing other than what we could see in the room — five babies; five cribs. Repeatedly Sister returned to the truth of the situation — her children, she said, are happy just to have food in their bellies.

Julia and I realized just how dire the situation was for these beautiful little children. Anxiety was welling up inside of me and I could tell Julia was sharing my own concern for the health and wellbeing of the infants. The Sisters were doing an amazing job in caring for the children, and against great odds, but quite simply, "More needs to be done," I thought.

I asked Sister where the newest baby at the home came from, and was told that her mother had given birth to her at a local hospital and, after the birth, asked to use the ladies room. Then the mother just walked out the front door of the hospital never to be seen again. The police had brought the baby to the children's home.

I asked why someone would abandon a newborn child. Father Stephen explained that this is common in cases of incest and rape. He also offered that these young mothers, who are not only victims of sexual assault but are also poor without any means of taking care of themselves or their babies, travel hundreds of miles to give birth in communities where no one knows them. Then they disappear from the hospitals and return to their homes. This way no questions are asked; it is as though the pregnancy and the baby had never happened.

The babies whose mothers are able to make it to a hospital to give birth are fortunate. They receive the care they need. But children who are born outside of the medical community are usually abandoned in the streets, or left on the doorsteps of churches. The police, and sometimes nuns and priests, try to find these children before they die from exposure to the elements. Some new mothers place their unwanted children in forests, where they know dogs and wild animals will surely kill them.

Horrified by these realities, Julia said she now understood why the children in the orphanage were so happy. They were safe and cared for. Before she arrived in Kenya, her Western sensibilities half imagined orphans being like those children portrayed in a Dicken's novel. She imagined orphans were sad little characters like Oliver Twist. In Kenya, orphans in children's homes know they are fortunate. They know that being in an orphanage is far better than the ugly alternatives. I, myself, hadn't fully understood the depth and breadth of the problem of these cast-off children until that moment when I stood in the infant room of the orphanage holding babies who were fortunate enough to survive the first perilous days of life and knowing that so many others had not. What must God think?

Near the babies' sleeping room was an empty play room that I imagined would soon be filled with more beds or cribs. I knew that Stephen was the trustee for four orphaned children, left behind when both of their parents died of AIDS. After the parents died, the children were given to distant relatives. When Stephen visited the children, he learned that they were being abused and used for child labor, so he removed them from those uncaring homes.

Stephen took the children out of their situations and arranged for a temporary alternative placement. I could tell he liked what he saw at this children's home and wondered if he was going to ask the Sisters to help him with the children left to his care. These Helpers of Mary are obviously kind, loving and hardworking women, facing what appeared to us to be insurmountable challenges as they cared for the children. Barely subsisting and stretched to the point of breaking, the Sisters stood on their faith, believing God would provide even in the darkest hours.

My Road to Kenya

Next we visited the older children who were waiting for us in the home's cafeteria. Sister Alphonsa took out a box of what appeared to be small orange balls. I thought they looked like oranges, but they were so small and brown spotted I couldn't be sure. I was fairly certain, however, that the orange balls were some kind of fruit; perhaps one I'd never seen before. Sister explained to the children that the "guests" were here to help pay their school fees; which we were. The smiling children all began talking at once, excitedly calling Julia "Auntie."

Mary Clare visits children at Holy Family Orphanage. Father Stephen joins Sister Alphonsa for a photo with the children.

Auntie is a term of deep respect in Kenya. An Auntie is a person, such as a family member, who helps children. It is disrespectful for a child to refer to an adult or a person of authority by his or her first name. The term Auntie is substituted in place of the person's given name. When Sister Alphonsa finished introducing us to the children, she asked Julia, Father Stephen and me to hand out treats, those orange and spotted balls I saw when I first entered the cafeteria. Holding one of the balls in my hand, I felt its soft, squishy texture and thought it odd. We handed out fifty-two orange balls to fifty-two waiting children and were startled to find we still had five hungry children, patiently sitting with no expression on their faces and no treat in their hands.

A look of panic flooded Sister Alphonsa's face. We realized she was embarrassed at not having enough treats for all the children, and especially so as this disaster was unfolding right in front of her guests. The other Sisters, quickly sizing up the situation, scrambled into action and began looking for something to give to the five empty-handed children. Eventually, the Sisters found five miniature bananas and handed them out to the waiting children.

I asked Stephen what kind of fruit we had given the children. He said they were indeed oranges just as I had thought. I asked how it is possible for oranges to be so small and brown, and he explained that it had been a bad season for oranges and the inferior fruit was all there was for the children to eat.

I told Sister Alphonsa I had some things I wanted to give to her. I went to my car and took out my laptop computer. I gave the computer to Sister for the children to use for watching Disney films. Before leaving, we asked Sister to make a list of needs for the orphanage and requested she meet us at Woolmat, a local store, early the next morning. We were going shopping! It was time for us to say our farewells and head back to our rooms for the night.

Back at Egerton University, Julia and I got to work making plans of our own for our shopping expedition the next day. We had Sister's list and we also had our own list created before we left home. And now, having seen with our own eyes the orphanage and the children, we realized there were many more pressing needs far beyond what we had originally thought when we were back in the United States preparing for the trip.

Once we had our lists compiled, checked and rechecked, we decided the needs could be organized into categories. We designated the need for food, hygiene items, and clothes and diapers as our "A" priorities. School supplies were put into the "B" category, and any "C" priorities we would leave to Sister Alphonsa to sort through. When we were finally through with our task, we ate our dinner and fell into bed exhausted.

Bright and early the following day we met Sister at the store. We each grabbed a cart and started shopping. The first items on our list were school supplies. Sister said the children needed paper and pencils. She seemed to be sorting out in her mind the exact number she needed for just the next day or two when Julia chirped in, saying, "Fifty-seven children need lots of notebooks and pencils," and began loading stacks of blue, green and pink notebooks into our shopping carts, almost filling one cart completely. She checked notebooks off the list and we moved on. The next stop was the toy section.

I asked if the children would like to have balls to play with. Sister picked up one ball and looked at me with the wide eyes of a child who was asking her mom for a toy, and said, "Is it okay if I have just one, please?" I picked up another, larger ball from the display and, taking the small ball Sister held in her hand, I placed them both in my shopping cart. Sister then cautiously picked up an air pump and looked at me in disbelief as I nodded "yes" and added the pump to the other toys in the cart. I quickly turned and headed down the aisle. Overcome by emotion at seeing the longing and appreciation on Sister's face, I couldn't allow myself to look back, afraid I would start crying right there in the middle of Woolmat's Toy Department.

Standing in front of a display of toy trucks, I mentioned to Sister that I thought boys liked toy trucks. She looked at one of the trucks with such longing in her eyes it pierced my heart. Julia and I grabbed a few of the trucks and added them to the cart.

Stephen, having a better understanding of his culture than Julia or I, said, "Gifts are for Christmas and special occasions." I realized my behavior in the toy section was very much atypical of the behavior that Kenyans would display. I took Stephen's cue and said I would agree to move on if we could just get something for the toddlers to sit on in the nursery are—a few bikes perhaps. He reminded me that bikes would not be helpful to Sister if she had no food for her hungry children. I understood. He was telling me to save my money for more important things. I also understood that by "other things" he was speaking of those items that could prove life saving for a small child.

Next we headed to the hygiene section. Julia asked what type of toothpaste the children used. Sister said that she always purchased the least expensive regardless of what item she might need. She wanted small containers of toothpaste for hygiene and health purposes. Julia determined the best price per ounce and piled tubes of toothpaste into the cart, and then declared that each child should also have a new toothbrush. Sister's eyes welled with tears and Father Stephen said he thought she seemed a bit overwhelmed by it all.

Julia and I decided independently of one another to stick to the list and not risk looking into Sister's eyes so that we could finish our task at hand without adding our own tears to the flood now coursing down Sister's cheeks. We simply had too much to do and too little time in which to do it. Aisle by aisle we navigated with speed, checking off items on our list as we made our way around the store.

The number of children orphaned by AIDS in Kenya is growing at an alarming rate. Taking this fact into account, we decided to up our estimate regarding the number of items needed at the children's home. We made the assumption there soon would be more orphaned children delivered to the home and so shopped accordingly.

Sister Alphonsa's voice began to crack from the flood of emotions springing up inside her, so we decided it would be best to keep our questions to a minimum, keeping both our attention and our eyes focused on our list.

Flying down the aisles as if wings were attached to our feet, we loaded soaps, cleansers, rice, diapers, Vaseline, tea, baby formulas, porridge, food stuffs and more into our already-brimming shopping carts. I wanted to purchase corn and a few treats as well, but Stephen informed me that corn could be purchased at other places at wholesale prices. He said treats were given out only on special occasions and asked me to put back the few cake mixes I was trying to sneak into my cart without his knowing. In the end, Julia and I nearly arm wrestled him to the ground so that we could get the children a few pieces of candy.

When we finally arrived at the checkout, our team of shoppers split up. I left Julia and Sister at the checkout while I led Stephen to the shop next door where we looked for a new toaster for Stephen's house. I had noticed during our visit that his toaster was missing.

I asked Stephen what had happened to his last toaster, and he said he had left it along with his microwave at the last house he had lived in. The house is now occupied by the Bishop, and Stephen, in his generosity, had left the appliances for the Bishop's own use.

While we shopped for the toaster, the cashiers at Woolmat were madly scanning and boxing the items for the children's home.

Stephen was in a hurry to move along, but our mission was not yet complete. I asked Sister to meet us at the local bank, explaining that we did not have time to purchase new clothes for the children and that she would have to complete this task on her own.

We went to the bank and deposited the money Sister would need to purchase the children's clothes and then handed her a small token of the gratitude we felt for her as she and the other Sisters give so much to care for the children at the home. We wanted her to have some money for her personal use. Julia smiled and said, "This will be our little secret." Then wishing her well, we asked her to stay in touch. As we drove away, Julia and I both knew this chapter in our love affair with Kenya was a long way from being closed.

As we end this book, construction on a new building at the orphanage is beginning. The building will house a kitchen, laundry and storage room.

All Roads Lead to Kenya. Julia stands at the base of a road sign which shows the distance Kenya is from major cities around the world, including London and New York City.

Appendix

Why We Do What We Do
Beautiful People and Wonderful Memories

Taking a break from the daily routine has given us time to write about some wonderful people, their accomplishments and contributions. We have shared many memorable experiences and good times, and much laughter along the way.

This is the first time we have documented the highlights of Jack's own leaky "Bucket List." We have enjoyed writing this book and hope the following list of completed projects will inspire others to take chances and reach out to help others fill their own buckets to full and overflowing.

Thank you,

Jack O'Leary and Mary Clare Lyons

Throughout the years, we were fortunate to be involved in so many projects in Kenya. I never planned to do any of it. It all just happened. These completed projects include:

1. Instituted St. John Fisher College Scholarships

Established a scholarship to educate Kenyan priests in the United States and to expose them to a working democracy. The goal was to educate and empower priests with leadership capabilities to make a difference in Kenya when they returned. As a result of the generosity of St. John Fisher College, the influence of the graduates has spread throughout much of East Africa. Six of the graduates have become Roman Catholic Bishops.

2. Completed a School Books Project

The initial project sent several pallets of books collected and organized by Mary Clare Lyons and her daughters, Julia and Kathleen. Initially, more than five-thousand textbooks were collected, sorted by class, grade level, and subject, and sent to Kenyan schools. An additional container of school supplies was sent to Father Simon's school in Kenya.

3. Built a Small Church for Father Stephen in Nakuru

Father Stephen Mbugua Ngari, PhD attended St. John Fisher College and RIT in the 1990s. The church that he grew up in as a child in Bahati, Kenya, was a dilapidated, mud-walled, thatched-roof structure. Despite its crumbling structure, members still faithfully attended Mass there. We built a new church to replace the original one in 1999.

4. Converted an English Farmhouse in Bahati into St. John's Cottage Hospital

An old one-story English farm house of about ten-thousand square feet was given to Father Stephen's parish on condition that it be converted into a hospital to support the community. We financed the conversion and, after it was completed, a forty-foot container of medical equipment to fully equip the hospital was shipped. It included a birthing center, an operating room, and a ward for women and children. Recent statistics show the child mortality rate in the area dropped a dramatic 80 percent since the hospital was built. These results were achieved primarily thanks to the facility's sterile birthing center. A decrease in infant and children deaths, as well as deaths of adults also was due to improved procedures for treating simple infections and dysentery.

5. Helped Equip a Tea Plantation Owned by the Archdiocese of Nairobi.

A tractor and irrigation equipment were furnished to revitalize a tea plantation owned by the Diocese of Nairobi. The project was planned and managed by Archbishop Rafael Ndingi, a St. John Fisher College graduate. The plantation currently employs one-hundred-and-fifty people and has expanded to include a dairy farm and vegetable fields, which furnish food for the local community. The surplus products are sold to the finest restaurants in Nairobi. Proceeds from the sale of these products supplies the Diocese with much needed funds for other projects.

6. Boguma: Expanded a Hospital Run by The Little Sisters of St. Francis in Boguma, Kenya

After the hospital was finished, we sent two containers of medical equipment to fully equip the hospital.

7. Rebuilt St. Paul's Hospital in Homa Bay, Kenya

St. Paul's Hospital was built in Homa Bay. The hospital staff primarily cares for women and children who suffer from HIV/AIDS. It is estimated that 50 percent of the population in this area of Homa Bay are HIV positive or suffer from AIDS. Again, a container of medical equipment was sent to furnish the hospital.

8. Built Industrial Chicken Coop and Cattle Barn

An industrial chicken coop was built for The Sisters of Saint Francis Novitiate. The eggs and milk help feed the novices who live there, and they sell the surplus for cash to support the novitiate.

9. Constructed Egerton University Multipurpose Building
A multipurpose building was constructed next to the university to house a kindergarten, small clinic, and a Neuman Center for students.

10. Hospital Revitalizations: Reequipped Approximately Twenty Healthcare Facilities
About twenty hospitals were reequipped and updated with needed supplies and equipment. First, professionals ascertained what equipment the hospitals required. Volunteers like Dr. Susan Crawford and nurse Sarah Brewin played key roles in completing needs analyses and inspecting the facilities prior to shipping containers of equipment.
The equipment was shipped as complete rooms, which included operating rooms, dental departments, libraries, birthing centers, waiting rooms, etc. In total, more than sixty different departments were shipped. A not-for-profit organization in North Andover, Massachusetts, named International Medical Equipment Cooperative (I.M.E.C.) collects and refurbishes used medical equipment. We purchased twenty containers from them and sent them to twenty hospitals in Kenya. The organization was founded and is managed by Tom Keefe.

11. Established Distribution Warehouse to Provide Consumable Medical Supplies
A warehouse outside of Nairobi, Kenya was leased. Each month a container of consumable medical supplies was sent to the warehouse. Most of the containers were purchased in Rochester, New York from an organization called Intervol, which is owned and managed by Dr. Ralph Pennino. Various hospitals and clinics in Kenya could then place orders at the warehouse via the Internet and then pick up the supplies at no charge. In all, eighty hospitals and healthcare facilities were supplied through the warehouse.

12. Completed First Orphanage for Handicapped Children.
A home for handicapped children was built to house one-hundred children. The home is dedicated to Sarah Ryan, deceased daughter-

in-law of Jim Ryan, Sr. and wife of Jim Ryan, Jr. Separate buildings were built to house a kitchen and a laundry at the orphanage. During the recent political unrest, the site became a refuge for more than one-thousand people who fled from danger to the site of the orphanage. Tents, fences, blankets, food, and other essentials were purchased to supply the refugees for a period of about fourteen months until it was safe for them to return home. The home was funded by the Ryan family, the Dorothea Haus Ross Foundation of Rochester, Mr. John Anderson, and Jack O'Leary.

13. Constructed St. John the Baptist Church.
St. John the Baptist Church is large enough to accommodate two-thousand parishioners at a time, and is dedicated to former president of St. John Fisher College Katherine Keough. For updated information and photographs of this project, visit www.myroadtokenya.com.

14. Helped Finance Homes for Handicapped Adults in Williamsburg, Virginia
The facilities are managed by Sister Agnes, a member of the Order of The Little Sisters of St. Francis. Her order is in Uganda near the western border of Kenya. She currently runs five homes for handicapped adults in the United States and, in November 2010, was licensed to run adult daycare programs in Virginia. Some of the profits from her business ventures are sent to her sisters to support the work of their mission. Sister Agnes' story was documented in 2010 and appears in downloadable form on the *My Road to Kenya* Website.

15. Nurses from St. John Fisher College Volunteer at Hospitals in Kenya
For more information on the Wegman's School of Nursing program in Kenya, you can read the story of the St. John Fisher College nursing experiences in Kenya written by Nancy Wilk at www.myroadtokenya.com. You also can contact St. John Fisher College directly at www.sjfc.edu.

For More Information, Contact:

Jack W. O'Leary
P.O. Box 387
Pittsford, New York 14534
Email addresses: joleary356@gmail.com or Myroadtokenya@gmail.com

To read more about our adventures in Kenya, visit us on Facebook at: MyRoadToKenya.
If you would like to learn more about I.M.E.C., you can contact Tom Keefe at Website: www.imecamerica.org Email:imec@imecamerica.org. The warehouse is staffed by Tom, his daughter, mother, and many helpers and superstar volunteers like Dr. Sue Crawford.

Special Thanks

Berfore completing this chapter of the journey, I would like to give special thanks to a number of individuals for whom I owe deep gratitude. Without these individuals'support, this book and these events would not have been possible.

Father George Akoth
Mr. John Anderson
Dr. Donald Bain
Basilian Fathers
Mr. Marty Birmingham, Sr.
Sr. Mary Brenda
Mr. Pat Burke, First Niagara Bank
Mrs. Sarah Brewin, RN
Mr. Doug Castner
Bishop Mathew Clark
Mrs. Amy Cole-Lang
Dr. Susan Crawford & Family
Dorothea Haus Ross Foundation, Rochester, NY
Mr. & Mrs. Ronald Fitzgerald
Mr. & Mrs. James Gonzales & Family
Mr. & Mrs. James Groh
Father Protus Hamisi
Mr. Tom Keefe & Family
Mrs. Megan Kelly & Family
Ms. Kathleen Kenning
Ms. Julia Kenning-Lyons
Dr. Katherine Keough & Family
Sr. Janet Korn
Kilian Schmitt Foundation

Loyola Foundation, Washington D.C.
Ms. Mary Ellen Masterpole
Father Stephen Mgbuma
Mrs. Maura Minges & Family
Bishop Rafael Ndingi
Dr. Bill O'Connor
Dr. Tim O'Connor
Mr. & Mrs. Brian O'Leary & Family
Mr. Dennis O'Leary and Family
Mr. & Mrs. John O'Leary, Jr. & Family
Ms. Kathleen O'Leary
Mr. Michael O'Leary & Family
Dr. R. Pennino & Friends of Intervol
Red Cross International
Dr. Gerry Rooney
Mr. Jim Ryan, Sr. & Family
Mr. Jim Ryan, Jr.& Family
St. John Fisher College
Mr. & Mrs. Frank Stotz & Family
Father Cleophas Tuka
Mr. & Mrs. Rob Turner & Family

Thank You

There is no passion to be found playing small, in settling for a life that is less than the one you are capable of living.
Nelson Mandela

Many American's have a vested interest in helping their friends in Kenya. We have forged long-lasting relationships and lifelong friendships that will sustain us all well into the future. More than a half century ago Father Charles Lavery made a commitment to assist his friends and, through them, the people of Kenya. Today this commitment continues to live and grow, turning his dream into a reality.

If you enjoyed reading these stories and wish to know more about our efforts and progress in Kenya, additional information can be found on the *MyRoadtoKenya.com* blog.

Thank you for giving me this opportunity to share with you this mission of hope that has filled my own heart with joy. Helping the people of Kenya continues to be very important to me, and I know it always will be.

Jack O'Leary

Afterward

Jack W. O'Leary is retired and lives in Western New York. He currently serves on the Board of The Diocese of Nakuru Special Fund, a 501(c)(3) corporation.

We wish to thank the many volunteer organizations and individuals who assisted in the completion of all the projects we've shared with you throughout this book.

We are grateful to be able to share our story with you. If *My Road to Kenya* inspires you to want to make a difference in the lives of our Kenyan friends, visit the www.myroadtokenya.com for more information, reviews, events, and information on travels and new projects.

If you enjoyed our story, we hope you will suggest *My Road to Kenya* to a colleague, friend, book club, men's or women's group, church, civic group, university or high school class, or any group interested in aiding children in Kenya.

Check to see if *My Road to Kenya* is in your local library or community center. If not, we would appreciate it if you could donate this book or suggest that they add a copy of *My Road to Kenya* to their collection.

You may wish to encourage your local independent bookstore or chain to carry this book, or ask the book reviewer of your local newspaper or radio station to consider reviewing this book to share the goodwill with their readers and listeners.

Epitaph

In order for evil to flourish, all that is required is for good men to do nothing. Edward Burke, British Philosopher and Statesman (1729-1797)

The hottest places in Hell are reserved for those who in time of great moral crises maintain their neutrality. Dante Alighieri Italian Poet, Prose Writer, Literary Theorist, Moral Philosopher, and Political Thinker (1265-1321)

The world turned a blind eye to the murder and mayhem that ravaged the country and violated the people of Kenya prior to and following the 2007 national elections. The violence left 1,500 persons murdered and hundreds of thousands of others homeless following a corrupted election process.

However, five years later, on January 23, 2012, the International Criminal Court (ICC) determined that it will pursue prosecution of four high-level Kenyan government officials accused of committing crimes of corruption, violence, and murder.

Those accused of financing, ordering and carrying out the atrocities include Kenya's finance minister and deputy prime minister, who has since resigned his post as finance minister, but continues in his post as deputy prime minister. He stands accused of funding election-related violence by providing $600,000 of the country's money for the purpose of affecting the outcome of the election and securing his own position of power. As of publication of this book, he has steadfastly maintained his innocence as well as his unofficial title as the richest man in Kenya.

Also as a result of the ICC's decision to prosecute individuals it deems responsible for the crimes, the cabinet secretary and head of civil service also has resigned. The former education minister, and a prominent radio journalist and member of Parliament were also charged by the ICC for their alleged roles in the violence. The actions of the ICC signal a change of direction in Kenya's long history of governmental corruption and election-related violence.

Ida Odinga, wife of Kenya's Prime Minister Raila Odinga, has called for a mechanism for trying the accused within Kenya. The recently ratified Kenyan constitution protects individual rights and liberties and is the cornerstone upon which an honest, democratic government will now be able to prevail against those who might seek to rule with impunity.

About the Authors

Jack O'Leary is an entrepreneur and philanthropist. In 1984, Jack, then corporate vice president of Burroughs Corporation, was approached to help launch International Imaging Materials, Inc. (IIMAK), which he took public one decade later.

While CEO and president of IIMAK, he was named campaign chairman for the United Way of Rochester, New York.

New York State's Entrepreneur of the Year in 1995, Jack retired from corporate life to enjoy more time with friends and family, including his eleven grandchildren.

He never intended to become involved in the lives of the people of Kenya, but having financed the education of several Kenyan students, he was invited to visit them. Soon he was refurbishing and building hospitals, clinics and orphanages, and undertaking other humanitarian projects.

Jack O'Leary

About Mary Clare Lyons

Mary Clare Lyons is one of four children born to Carol and Charles B. Kenning of Rochester, New York. She retired from corporate America in 1995 to raise her two daughters and teach at Pittsford Mendon High School.

As a teacher, she had the opportunity to be the faculty advisor for a community service

Mary Clare Lyons

club wherein she worked on several projects with local charities. She travelled to Kenya for the first time in 2007, falling in love with the people, the country's rich and diverse history, and its breath-taking landscapes.

Today, Mary Clare divides her time between New York and Florida while continuing her efforts to grow and fulfill her passion for learning.

CPSIA information can be obtained at www.ICGtesting.com
Printed in the USA
BVOW031701100912

300062BV00002B/3/P